the 4x4 COOKBOOK

the 4x4 COOKBOOK

RITA VAN DYK

With gratitude to Izak Barnard of Penduka Safaris
who allowed me to cook for his clients and who
taught me so much; and to Johan who always supports
and encourages me in whatever I do.

Struik Publishers (Pty) Ltd
(a member of Struik New Holland Publishing (Pty) Ltd)
Cornelis Struik House
80 McKenzie Street
Cape Town 8001

Reg. No.: 1954/000965/07

First published in 2000
10 9 8 7 6 5 4 3 2

Publishing manager: Linda de Villiers
Editor: Joy Clack
Cover designer: Loretta Steyn
Designer: Lellyn Creamer
Proofreader: Proofread cc
Indexer: Brenda Brickman

Reproduction by Hirt & Carter Cape (Pty) Ltd
Printed and bound by CTP Book Printers (Pty) Ltd

ISBN 1 86872 422 0

The information on haybox cooking is adapted from
The South African Backpacker by Helmke Hennig
(published by Purnell and Sons (SA) (Pty) Ltd, 1978)
with kind permission from the author.

Contents

Planning and Preparation

COOKING AND BAKING

Camp stoves

The most popular camp stove is one that uses butane gas for fuel under its one, two or three burners. In many cases a gas stove admirably solves the cooking problem and it is a good solution in times when firewood is not available. It is also handy for short lunch stops when you don't want to make a fire just to prepare tea. Pots and pans don't burn black on a gas stove as they do on an open fire, and are therefore easier to clean.

Dutch oven

This is a black, heavy, flat-bottomed cast-iron casserole with a lid (also known as a 'potjie'), which can be used on top of the fire for casseroles as well as for baking breads and preparing other dishes. It is very versatile and an essential item on any safari.

To bake a dish, place the ingredients in the greased pot (grease the inside of the lid too) and place the pot on a low grid over a bed of moderate coals. Put a sheet of foil over the pot before putting on the lid (the foil should be larger than the diameter of the pot) to prevent ash getting into the food. Heap additional coals on top of the lid. After about 30 minutes, remove the coals on top and lift the lid. If the dish doesn't seem to be cooking fast enough, add more live coals on top of the lid. Be careful not to put too many hot coals under the pot, but rather increase the heat on top of the lid by adding more coals, as the dish is more likely to burn if you have hot coals underneath.

The temperature of the coals will depend on the type of wood (and the quantity) you use. Experience is the only way you can determine the time a dish needs to bake. For instance, bread takes quite some time to bake and is best cooked underground. To do this, dig a hole somewhat larger than the pot and fill it with a blazing hardwood fire. When the blaze has burned down to coals, shovel out about half of them. Put the pot in the hole and ease it around until it is evenly settled. Rake the embers back in until the whole pot, except for the handle, is hidden. Once again, experience is needed to know how long the bread takes to bake, and it depends on the amount and quality of coals used. It is therefore recommended that you experiment at home a few times before setting out on safari.

Other ways to bake food

Several new inventions for baking food have become available in recent years. Some of these are: kettle grills, available as charcoal or gas kettles (some models are portable with detachable legs and weigh only 2 kg); mini braai ovens (which can be used over a gas cylinder with a normal cooking-plate attachment, and which also have collapsible legs to allow for easy transportation); and convection pans and pots (which can be used either over gas or on the open fire). For the purpose of this book, the Dutch oven has been used to test recipes, but you may well prefer one of the newer inventions.

Haybox cooking

The principle of this method is that the pot is insulated against heat loss so that the food is cooked slowly in its own heat. The apparatus needed for this cooking method is found in most safari vehicles: saucepan, dishcloth or towel, large plastic bag, thermal blanket or piece of aluminium foil and a sleeping bag. (An alternative to the plastic bag and thermal blanket is to use the inside of a winebox, provided the saucepan is small enough to fit inside. Remove the bag from the winebox, remove the tap and slit the bag open on one side.)

Method:
1. Bring food to the boil. Do not lift the lid or peep at the food before wrapping it up, as you need to retain the heat and steam in the pot. It is essential that the wrapping be done as quickly as possible so that minimal heat is lost.
2. Take the pot off the heat, quickly wrap it in the dishcloth or towel and put it into a plastic bag (to prevent moisture reaching the sleeping bag). When cooking over an open fire, use a cloth or towel specifically for this purpose, as it will become black from the soot on the pot. The thermal blanket or foil is wrapped around next with the reflecting surface closest to the pot. Lastly, fold the sleeping bag several times around the pot.
3. Leave the food to cook for about 1 hour or more. The food can be left for a longer time, but it will become cold if left too long as the wraps do not insulate it as thoroughly as would a proper haybox.

The haybox method is recommended for several reasons:

❖ You can prepare the food within a few minutes and then go off sightseeing or swimming, and come back to a lovely hot meal.
❖ Soups, stews (especially those prepared with soya mince), casseroles, dried vegetables, rice and fruit stews are all worthy subjects for haybox cooking. It is not necessary to soak dehydrated foodstuffs before cooking when using the haybox method. It is also ideal for preparing a complete meal in one pot. With a little ingenuity you can adapt any of your favourite casserole dishes to haybox cooking.

❖ The flavour of the food is much improved by the extended, slow cooking time.

❖ The food doesn't burn and you don't have to worry about scouring the pot afterwards.

❖ It saves gas when fuel supplies are running low.

How to cook dehydrated vegetables

Dried vegetables are usually more tender if they have been soaked long enough to reabsorb most of their lost moisture. If they are placed directly into a boiling soup or stew and are cooked without being given time to plump, they will be tougher.

Use only as much water as is necessary to cover the vegetables. Boiling water shortens the rehydration time, but cold water can also be used. Soak the vegetables for about 30 minutes to 1 hour. After rehydration the vegetables will be ready to be cooked. Simmered vegetables will be more tender than those cooked over high heat.

Vegetables can also be prepared according to the haybox cooking method, saving time as you combine the soaking and cooking time (*see* haybox cooking on page 7).

EQUIVALENTS

The following list shows the equivalent weight in grams or millilitres of 1 cup for various foodstuffs:

Beans, dried	250 g
Cheese, grated	125 g
Cocoa	111 g
Coconut, desiccated	75 g
Cornflour	166 g
Margarine	250 g
Mealiemeal, unsifted	166 g
Milk	250 ml
Oats	91 g
Plain (cake) flour	125 g
Raisins	188 g
Rice, uncooked	250 g
Sugar, white	250 g
Water	250 ml

PACKING FOOD AND EQUIPMENT

Plastic bags are ideal for packaging dry mixes such as cereals, dried fruit, dried beans or nuts. They leave the contents visible from the outside. During very rough going they must be protected from abrasion and puncturing. The bags can be sealed with adhesive cellulose tape or a rubber band.

Lightweight, unbreakable plastic bottles with screwtops are available on the market. You can use these to store cooking oil and other liquids. Wide-necked bottles can be used to store margarine, which won't leak if it turns soft in hot weather, especially when cooling facilities are unavailable.

Don't throw away the containers in which eggs are bought. Leave the eggs in their containers and pack them tightly and snugly into a larger container. As you use the eggs, place the empty cartons back in the bottom of the bigger container so that the remaining eggs do not shake around while travelling.

Food and equipment should be packed in sturdy, square (easier to pack than round ones) trunks to withstand the rigours of rough travelling. Wrap breakables such as glasses in plastic bubble wrap (obtainable from stationery shops) instead of newspaper, which becomes soggy when it gets wet.

How much of each

No one can tell you how much to take of various items. It all depends on the number of meals you expect to make of each kind of food, how many there are in the party and how much of each particular nutriment it will take to make a satisfying portion for each individual concerned. To determine quantities, you should experiment during weekend camping trips, preferably with the people that will be going on safari with you. Remember, the success of a safari depends on how well it is planned.

Cans

Use a water-resistant pen to write the contents on top of the can in case the labels wash off in the rain.

Instead of puncturing the lids of tins such as evaporated milk, make small openings on opposite sides just below the rim. You can then seal them easily with a wide elastic band to prevent the contents from spilling when you travel.

The lunchbox

It is useful to pack a lunchbox before breaking camp in the morning. Pack the kettle, firegrid (or gas bottle), etc. so that it is easily accessible during the lunch stop or tea-break. Easier still, prepare coffee or tea in a thermos flask, but be aware that it will most probably be finished before lunchtime!

Sandwiches, fruit and a salad make a light but satisfying lunch. Pack extra fruit and a box of biscuits in the vehicle for snacks, as well as a bottle of fresh water for each person. Also keep a clean rubbish bag in the vehicle to prevent littering. To keep the lunchbox cool and to have water available for sundowners, freeze a 1-litre bottle (the ones in which you buy milk or fruit juice) of water overnight and use it instead of ice packs. They stay frozen for longer, and when they defrost you have ice-cold water to drink.

Fats

Take along margarine and not butter, as milk-based products quickly turn rancid in hot weather. Hard margarine will also keep better than soft margarine, but if a cooler box or refrigerator is available this does not need to be considered.

THE OPEN FIRE

Regulating heat

When cooking over an open fire, different degrees of heat can be obtained by either building a fire with lots of flames (for frying and quick boiling) or by allowing the fire to burn down to form coals. Some coals can then be scraped to one side to provide low heat for simmering and keeping food warm.

Safety
Never kindle a fire on surfaces made up of decomposed or living vegetation. When you leave a camp, put out the fire by saturating it with water. Do not throw dishwater out when breaking up camp, but use it to clean your hands after everything has been packed and then douse the fire with the water.

Make sure you know which wood is poisonous, such as tamboti, and which wood gives an unpleasant taste to the food, such as pine.

WATER

Availability
In some wilderness areas water is not readily available and provision must therefore be made to take along your own water in plastic containers. It is also a good idea to refill all the water containers whenever water is available. Even where water is readily available, it is essential always to have enough in the vehicle for emergency situations. Each person should have their own water bottle, preferably an insulated one, in the vehicle.

Purifying
The easiest way to sterilize water is to boil it for at least 5 minutes. Water purification tablets can also be used and are available from outdoor shops.

Cooling
Water-cooling bags are ideal for cooling water on safari. They are slightly porous so that a little fluid continually seeps through and wets the outside. This exterior moisture evaporates in the air and so lowers the interior temperature of the bag. Hanging the bag in a breeze may speed up the process.

You can also purify the water at the same time by dropping in water purification tablets.

REMINDER LIST OF WHAT TO PACK
The following list serves as a guideline only and should be adapted to suit individual needs. Do not pack everything on this list unless you own a 10-tonne truck!

Learn to be selective and go on weekend camping trips beforehand to determine what your personal needs are – the secret of a successful safari is to pack as few items as possible without compromising essentials and comfort.

Clothes
1 set of smart-casual clothes
Balaclava and gloves (in winter)
Cotton hat or cap
Long-sleeved cotton shirts if you
    are sensitive to the sun
Sandals
Shorts
Short-sleeved cotton shirts or
    T-shirts
Swimwear
Tracksuit
Underwear
Walking shoes and socks
Warm jacket
Waterproof suit or jacket

Toiletries

Hair brush
Shampoo
Lip salve
Mirror
Nail brush
Nail clipper
Plug (to fit bath and washbasin)
Razor and extra blades
Sanitary pads and/or tampons
Shaving foam and after-shave lotion
Small needle-and-thread kit
Soap
Sponge or face cloth
Tissues
Toilet paper
Toothbrush
Toothpaste
Towel

First aid

Antihistamine
Antiseptic lotion
Aspirin
Bandages and dressings
Copy of prescription (if any)
   from doctor
Cotton wool
Eye and ear drops
Germolene® salve
Imodium® or other medication
   for diarrhoea
Insect repellent (citronella candles,
   mosquito coils, mosquito spray)
Malaria tablets
Muscle salve
Personal/prescription medication
Plasters
Space blanket
Sunburn soother
Sunscreen
Throat lozenges
Travel-sickness tablets

General

Batteries (for torch, camera, video
   and other equipment)
Binoculars
Bucket with lid
Camera and extra film
Cellularphone and charger
   (arrange for international
   roaming, if applicable)
Credit card (arrange for emergency
   funds)
Compass (GPS)
Cooler box and/or refrigerator
Daypack (for short walks)
Dustpan and brush
Field guides, maps, travel guides
   and other books
Flashlight with spare batteries
Games (cards, etc.)
Gas lamp, or other source of light
Generator
Locks (for trailer and tent)
Masking/insulation tape
Medical insurance documentation
   (make sure international
   emergencies are covered)
Moonbag® (to carry passports,
   money and other valuables)
Notebook and pen
Pocket knife
Pratley's® putty
Ratchet ties
Receipts/documents for bookings
Scissors
Spectacles
Sturdy trunks (to pack equipment
   and food)
Sunglasses
Washing line and pegs
Washing powder for laundry
Water bottles (preferably insulated)
   to keep with you during the day
Water containers with water

Border post

Car registration papers
Driver's licences of all drivers
(international licence, if
applicable)
Foreign currency
Identity document
List of equipment serial numbers
(binoculars, cameras, etc.)
Passport
Pen
Trailer registration papers
Visa

Camping equipment

Awning or canvas for shade and
rain (remember poles and pegs)
Camp beds/foam or inflatable
mattresses
Folding chairs and table
Ground sheet
Hammer
Mosquito net
Pillows
Portable shower (or plastic
washbasin)
Sleeping bags
Tent (remember the tent poles
and pegs)

For the fire

Axe/hatchet
Braai grid
Firelighters
Long fork and spoon
Matches in waterproof containers
(i.e. film canisters)
Metal tongs
Small saw or chopper

For the vehicle

Clutch and brake fluid
Condensers (if applicable)

Emergency triangles (for vehicle
as well as trailer)
Engine oil
Exhaust repair kit
Fan belts
Fire extinguisher
Folding spade
Fuel filter
Full set of tools
Fuses
Hand cleaner and cloth
Hand-held spotlight
Jack and/or hi-lift jack
Jerrycans (with spare fuel)
and funnel
Jumper leads
Light bulbs
Lubricating oil
Maps
Points (if applicable)
Puncture repair kit
Radiator hoses and clamps
Regulator
Spare set of keys
Spare tyres for vehicle and trailer
Spark plugs
Tie ropes/straps
Tow rope
Tyre levers
Tyre pressure gauge
Tyre pump (with fittings
for inflatable mattresses,
if applicable)
Wheel spanner
Wire (to fix things temporarily)

For the kitchen

2 sponges or dishcloths
3 drying cloths
Aluminium foil
Bottle and can opener
Bread knife
Chopping board

Cling wrap
Coffee mugs
Cooker top for gas stove
Corkscrew
Cutlery (knives, forks, teaspoons, tablespoons, serving spoons)
Dishwashing liquid
Egg lifter
Gas bottle (remember the key) with extensions
Glasses or stainless steel tumblers
Grater
Hand mixer/whisk
Jaffle iron
Kettle
Large elastic bands (to close open bags of sugar, etc.)
Large frying pan (if large group)
Measuring spoons and jug
Oven gloves
Paper napkins
Paper towels
Plastic bags, small and large (to store left-overs)
Plastic bottles (not round) to freeze water and use in cooler box
Plastic bowls of various sizes, with lids
Plates and porridge/pudding bowls
Potato masher (or use a fork)
Potato peeler
Rubbish bags (all rubbish, including the bags, must be carried out of wilderness areas)
Saucepans of various sizes (heavy cast-iron if cooking over open fire)
Screw-top jars
Serving bowls
Sharp vegetable knife
Small frying pan
Steel wool and/or scouring pads
Table cloth
Trays (if you can't eat on your lap or at a table)
Vacuum flask
Washbasin (if taking another one for washing yourself, take two different colours to differentiate)
Water bottles
Wooden spoon

Food (make your own selection from this list)
Baking powder
Bicarbonate of soda
Biltong, dried wors and salami
Bottled sauces
Bread
Breakfast cereals
Canned beans
Canned fruit
Canned meat and fish
Canned tomatoes and tomato purèe
Canned vegetables
Cheese
Cheese spread
Chocolates
Chutney
Cocoa and other hot drinks
Coffee
Condensed milk
Cooking oil and olive oil
Cornflour
Curry powder
Dehydrated vegetables
Desiccated coconut
Dried fruit
Dried yeast
Eggs
Evaporated milk
Fresh fruit (lemons, oranges, naartjies, bananas, apples, water melon, pineapple, papaya, etc.)

Fresh meat and bacon, vacuum-packed (check the regulations regarding fresh meat before taking any across borders)

Fresh vegetables (potatoes, onions, pumpkins, tomatoes, cabbages, avocados, butternuts, carrots, beans, green peppers, garlic, cucumbers, etc.)

Fruit juice

Gherkins

Instant desserts

Instant packet sauces

Instant mashed potato

Jams, honey, peanut butter and other spreads

Jelly powder

Liquor (remember restrictions at border posts)

Long-life cream

Long-life custard (or custard powder)

Long-life milk and milk powder

Long-life yoghurt

Margarine

Marshmallows

Mayonnaise

Mealiemeal

Mussels, canned

Mustard, powder and prepared

Nuts

Olives

Pepper

Plain (cake) flour

Popcorn

Powdered cooldrinks

Raisins

Rice

Rolled oats

Rusks

Salt

Savoury biscuits

Selection of herbs and spices

Self-raising flour

Soup, cans and packets

Soy sauce

Spaghetti and other pasta

Stock cubes

Sugar, white and brown

Sweet biscuits

Tea

Tomato sauce

Vinegar

Worcestershire sauce

INSTANT MEALS

The following instant foods are suggestions for those meals where you are unable to, or do not want to cook. The purpose of this section is not to be complete, but rather to set you thinking and to make you aware of the possibilities of the items that are readily available on supermarket shelves. New items appear on the shelves every day, so to make life easier for yourself, be a 'supermarket-junkie' before you pack for the safari and buy a few ready-prepared meals.

Breakfast

1. Breakfast cereals: For each serving, mix 1 cup cereal with 2 teaspoons sugar and 1 tablespoon milk powder and hot or cold water to taste. The milk powder and water can of course be replaced by fresh or long-life milk, if available.

2. Granola bars, rusks: with coffee.

3. Instant oats: The secret is to add enough water to the oats to ensure that the mixture isn't

sticky. A chopped banana on top adds a fresh touch.

4. Long-life yoghurt: It can be kept at room temperature for up to three months.

Lunch

1. Processed meat or canned meat.
2. Smoked mussels or canned liver pâté (available at delicatessens) on savoury biscuits.
3. Fruit rolls and fresh fruit.
4. Canned or bottled salads, such as three-bean salad or beetroot.

Dinner

1. Instant pasta and sauce.
2. Chinese noodles with tuna.
3. Instant savoury and sweet sauces.
4. Cook-in-the-bag rice.
5. Instant spicy sauces over meat.
6. Instant mashed potato: can also be used to thicken sauces.
7. Bacon bits (bacon-flavoured soya): add to soups and dinners.
8. Lentils: nutritious and lightweight. Cook according to the haybox method (see page 7) with rice and curry powder for a hassle-free, nutritious meal.
9. Cheese- or meat-filled tortellini and ravioli (dried).
10. Irradiated food can be obtained from the Atomic Energy Corporation in Pretoria. The food does not need to be refrigerated and once rehydrated, tastes (almost) like the fresh product.

Desserts

1. Long-life custard and cream.
2. Vanilla crème caramel instant pudding.
3. Instant chocolate mousse.
4. Instant milk tart, mousse cake.
5. Roast marshmallows over the fire or a candle flame.
6. Mix instant pudding with full-cream milk powder and water (1½ cups cold water to 3 tablespoons milk powder) or fresh milk. Add coconut, chocolate, chopped nuts or dried fruit.
7. Pack sweet biscuits in a container and pour over chocolate or any other favourite liqueur. Serve with custard.
8. Simply open a packet of Albany Tinkies®.
9. Add custard and/or a can of fruit to muesli.
10. Mix cornflakes with condensed milk (or instant custard) for a sweet treat.
11. Soak prunes in brandy for an hour or two and serve with custard or a small can of cream or evaporated milk.

Snacks

1. Dried fruit: figs, pineapple, apricots, mebos, minced fruit cubes, minced fruit croquettes, fruit rolls, fruit chips.
2. Mix nuts with raisins and candy-covered chocolate.
3. Energy bars and tropical chewy bars.
4. Biltong and dried wors.
5. Crisps, cheese curls and bacon streaks.

Breakfast

Muesli base
(to be prepared at home)
Serves 8–10

5 cups jumbo rolled oats
4 cups rolled wheat
4 cups rolled barley
4 cups rolled rye

Thoroughly mix the cereals together. Store in an airtight container. Nuts, seeds and dried fruit can be added to taste when on safari. Serve with hot or cold milk.

Fruit and nut muesli
(to be prepared at home)
Serves 10

½ cup sunflower seeds
½ cup chopped dried apricots
½ cup chopped dates
½ cup chopped almonds
½ cup chopped walnuts
3 cups rolled oats

Toast the sunflower seeds in a pan and mix all ingredients with the oats. Store in an airtight container. Serve with hot or cold milk.

Basic granola
(to be prepared at home)
Serves 24

2 cups whole-wheat flour
6 cups rolled oats
1 cup desiccated coconut
1 cup wheat germ
1 tablespoon salt
½ cup water
1 cup oil
½ cup golden syrup or honey
2 teaspoons vanilla essence

Combine dry ingredients in one bowl and liquid ingredients in another. Add liquid to dry ingredients and mix thoroughly. Spread on two greased baking sheets and bake for 1 hour at 120 °C (250 °F) or until golden-brown and dry. Store in a covered container. A variety of dried fruits, nuts and seeds can be added. Serve with hot or cold milk.

Weetbix® and apples
Serves 4

4 apples, cored and grated
  (do not peel)
2 Weetbix® biscuits, flaked
1 cup seedless raisins
1 cup apple juice
1 cup yoghurt
1 cup chopped nuts
4 tablespoons brown sugar

Spoon apples into a dish and top
with Weetbix®. Sprinkle with
raisins. Mix apple juice and
yoghurt and pour over the mixture.
Sprinkle nuts and sugar on top.

Oats porridge
Serves 4

4–5 cups water
1 teaspoon salt
1 cup oats
1 cup seedless raisins

Bring salted water to the boil.
Mix oats with a little cold water
and add to the boiling water. Stir
continuously until mixture starts
to thicken. Add raisins and simmer
gently for 15 minutes. Serve with a
little hot or cold milk.

VARIATION
Add 1 cup condensed milk to the
porridge about 5 minutes before it is
removed from the fire.

Mealie meal porridge (Stywe pap)
Serves 6

4 cups water
2 teaspoons salt
2 tablespoons margarine
  (optional)
2½ cups mealie meal

Bring salted water and margarine
to the boil. Slowly pour in mealie
meal, stirring vigorously with a
wooden spoon to prevent lumps.
Cover saucepan and place pot
over low heat to steam for about
1 hour. Stir from time to time.
  Serve with sugar and milk for
breakfast, or with a braaipap
sauce (see page 92) as a side dish
with meat.

VARIATION
1 cup grated Cheddar cheese
1 x 410 g can corn kernels
1 x 250 g packet bacon, cut
  into small pieces and fried
  until crisp
1 onion, chopped and fried
  until golden

Stir all ingredients into pap until
cheese has melted. Serve with
sausages and eggs as a side dish.

Porridge
Serves 4

5–6 cups water
1 teaspoon salt
1 cup mealie meal

Bring salted water to the boil.
Mix mealie meal with a little cold
water to form a paste and stir into
boiling water until porridge starts
to thicken. Allow to simmer very
slowly for about 20 minutes. Serve
hot with milk and sugar.

Porridge pizza
Serves 4

Porridge (see recipe above)

TOPPING
2 onions, finely chopped
1 x 250 g packet bacon, diced
margarine
4 tomatoes, finely chopped
1 x 285 g can creamed
  mushrooms
salt and pepper to taste
1 cup grated Cheddar cheese

Put a layer of the porridge in
a fireproof dish and leave for
30 minutes to set. Fry onions and
bacon in margarine. Add tomatoes
and mushrooms and simmer for
10 minutes. Season well. Pour over
porridge and sprinkle with cheese.
Cover with aluminium foil (shiny
side towards food) and place over
low heat until cheese has melted.

Welsh rarebit
Serves 2

1 tablespoon margarine
1 tablespoon flour
½ teaspoon salt
½ teaspoon mustard powder
1 cup warm milk
½ cup grated Cheddar cheese
4 slices bread, toasted on grid
  over hot coals

Melt margarine over low heat
and add flour, salt and mustard.
Gradually mix in warm milk and
stir continuously for 5 minutes.
Add cheese and stir until melted.
Spoon over toast and serve
immediately.

French toast
Serves 4–6

2 eggs, beaten
1 cup milk
¼ teaspoon salt
8 slices bread
¼ cup margarine

Mix eggs, milk and salt and dip
both sides of the bread in the
mixture. Melt margarine and fry
bread on both sides until golden-
brown. Serve with honey, syrup,
cinnamon sugar or tomato sauce.

Fried sandwiches
Serves 4

8 slices bread
margarine
4 slices Cheddar cheese
4 slices canned ham
2 eggs
4 tablespoons milk
salt and pepper to taste
oil for frying

Spread the bread with margarine and sandwich together with a slice of cheese and a slice of ham. Beat eggs with milk and season with salt and pepper. Dip sandwiches in the egg mixture and fry in hot oil for about 3 minutes on each side.

Other delicious fillings for fried sandwiches (also suitable for a light lunch or dinner):
* Fried bacon and mushroom
* Salami and apple
* Sardines with a little lemon juice
* Chicken and herbs
* Prawn and ham (canned)
* Apple and blue cheese
* Curried chicken
* Cottage cheese and bacon
* Banana and brown sugar
* Cream cheese and jam
* Apple and ground cinnamon
* Apple, chopped raisins and honey
* Pineapple and cheese

* Tomato and ham
* Scrambled eggs with chopped gherkins
* Grated cheese with a little chopped onion
* Grated cheese with chutney
* Fried mushrooms with a little tomato paste
* Cheese, tomato and onion
* Chicken and mayonnaise
* Onion, bacon, green pepper and tomato
* Minced meat
* Banana, ham, cheese and garlic

Spanish tortilla
Serves 4

1 large potato, cooked
1 small onion
1 tablespoon oil
3 eggs
1 tablespoon water
salt and pepper to taste

Peel and dice the potato and chop the onion. Heat the oil and brown the vegetables, stirring now and then. Beat the eggs lightly with the water. Season. Pour into pan with onion and potato. Let the eggs begin to set, tilting the pan and lifting the mixture so that the egg will run underneath and cook. When the bottom is set, turn the omelette over and cook the other side.

Orange bread
Serves 6–8

2 eggs, beaten
2 tablespoons castor sugar
1 teaspoon ground cinnamon
1 cup orange juice
2 teaspoons grated orange rind
10 slices bread
3 tablespoons margarine
honey

Mix eggs, castor sugar, cinnamon, orange juice and rind. Dip bread in mixture and fry both sides in melted margarine until golden-brown. Serve with honey.

Mozzarella sardine rolls
Serves 4

4 soft breadrolls
margarine
4 slices mozzarella cheese
2 x 120 g cans sardines in oil, drained
salt and pepper to taste
grated rind of 1 lemon

Cut breadrolls in half and spread with margarine. Arrange cheese and whole sardines on one half of each roll. Season and sprinkle with lemon rind. Close rolls, wrap in foil and place on a grid over hot coals until cheese has melted.

Bacon and mushroom dish
Serves 6–8

2 x 250 g packets bacon
4 tablespoons margarine
8 eggs, beaten
1½ cups milk
1 teaspoon salt
½ teaspoon pepper
1 x 285 g can creamed mushrooms
1 cup grated Cheddar cheese

Fry bacon in margarine until crisp. Remove bacon from pan and set aside. Beat eggs, milk, salt and pepper together and stir-fry in pan in which bacon was fried. Add bacon and mushrooms and mix well with eggs. Sprinkle with cheese. Serve immediately.

HANDY HINT
To brown the top of a dish or to melt cheese, heat a metal sheet and carefully place it on top of the dish, taking care not to get any sand or dirt into the food.

Soup

Smoked mussel soup

Serves 6

1 x 305 g can condensed
  chicken soup
2 x 105 g cans smoked mussels,
  drained and mashed
1 tomato, peeled, seeded and
  chopped
1½ cups milk
1½ cups water
1 cup cream
½ teaspoon dried mixed herbs
4 tablespoons plain (cake) flour
2 tablespoons dry sherry
  (optional)
pinch of sugar
salt and pepper to taste

Bring soup, mussels, tomato,
milk and water to the boil, then
remove from heat. Stir cream
and herbs into flour and add
to soup mixture. Stir over low
heat until hot, but not boiling.
Remove from heat and add
sherry, sugar and seasoning.
(A 48 g packet chicken soup
may be used instead of the canned
soup. In this case, leave out the
milk, water and flour and prepare
according to the instructions on
the packet, which includes a longer
cooking time, before adding the
other ingredients.)

Butternut soup

Serves 6

1 small butternut, peeled and
  cut into small pieces
enough water to just cover
  butternut
1 teaspoon salt
1 teaspoon curry powder
1 teaspoon ground ginger
pinch of pepper
1 cup cream, evaporated milk
  or full-cream milk

Cook butternut with all other
ingredients, except the cream,
until soft. Drain, but reserve water.
Mash butternut very well and add
reserved cooking water. Mix well.
Cook for a few minutes to reduce
and blend the liquid a little. Add
cream and allow to heat through.
A dash of orange juice may be
added, if desired (be careful not
to add too much or the cream
will curdle).

Cheese and rice soup
Serves 2

1 onion, chopped
1 tablespoon margarine
1 tablespoon plain (cake) flour
¼ teaspoon salt
1 teaspoon prepared mustard
1 cup water
1 cup milk
4 tablespoons cooked rice
2 tablespoons grated Cheddar
  cheese

Fry the onion in the margarine until golden. Add the flour, salt and mustard, then fry for a further 2 minutes. Add the water and stir until the mixture thickens. Simmer 10 minutes more. Add the milk and rice and bring to the boil. Remove from heat, add the cheese, and stir until cheese has melted.

Cream of sweetcorn soup
Serves 2–3

1 tablespoon margarine
1 tablespoon plain (cake) flour
½ cup chicken stock
salt and pepper to taste
1 tablespoon Worcestershire
  sauce
1 cup canned creamed
  sweetcorn
¼ cup cream or evaporated milk
1 teaspoon dried parsley

Melt margarine in a saucepan. Stir in the flour and cook for a few minutes. Remove from heat and gradually stir in the stock, seasoning and Worcestershire sauce. Bring gently to the boil, then remove from heat. Stir the sweetcorn into the pan. Bring back to the boil and simmer gently for 8 minutes. Stir the cream or milk into the soup and sprinkle with parsley.

Home-made dry soup mix
(to be prepared at home)

1 cup milk powder
1 cup nutritional yeast
1 cup soybean flour
¼ cup dried mixed herbs

Blend all ingredients and store in an airtight container. To prepare the soup when on safari, use 6 tablespoons of this mix to 2 cups water per serving and bring to the boil. Dried peas and beans, barley, lentils or other dried legumes and cereals may also be ground and added to the soup mix.

Fish

Portuguese sandwiches
Serves 4

8 slices bread
margarine
1 x 120 g can sardines in oil,
  drained and mashed
1 green apple, cored, peeled
  and grated
1 onion, finely chopped
3 tablespoons mayonnaise
½ teaspoon lemon juice
pinch each of mustard powder
  and pepper
4 tomatoes, sliced
¼ teaspoon salt

Spread the bread with margarine.
Mix the sardines, apple and onion
with the mayonnaise, lemon juice,
mustard and pepper to a smooth
consistency and spread this on
four slices of bread. Arrange the
sliced tomatoes on top and
sprinkle with salt. Top with
remaining bread slices and wrap
each sandwich in foil. Place the
sandwiches on a grid over hot
coals and grill for 5 minutes on
each side. Carefully remove the foil
and toast the sandwiches on each
side until lightly browned.

Basque sardines
Serves 4

2 onions, chopped
1 green pepper, seeded and
  sliced
4 tomatoes, sliced
salt and pepper to taste
2 x 120 g cans Portuguese
  sardines in oil
2 hard-boiled eggs

Fry onions and green pepper in
oil drained from the sardine cans.
When soft, add tomatoes and
seasoning and cook for another
3 minutes. Add sardines and
simmer slowly until dish is
warmed through. Garnish with
egg slices and serve with bread.

HANDY HINT
To revive wilted vegetables, simply
soak them in cold water for an hour
or more. A little lemon juice may be
added if desired. Overripe tomatoes
can be given new life by soaking
them in a bowl of cold water to
which a little salt and lemon juice
have been added.

Paella
Serves 4–6

1 onion, chopped
1 green pepper, seeded and
   chopped
1 x 285 g can mushrooms,
   drained
1 x 410 g can peas, drained
1 x 225 g can black olives,
   stoned
1 x 210 g can tuna
2 cups rice, uncooked
4 cups water
1 x 32 g packet instant
   chilli sauce
1 x 105 g can smoked mussels
salt and pepper to taste

Heat oil drained from the cans
of tuna and mussels and fry
onion and green pepper in it.
Add mushrooms, peas, olives,
tuna, rice, water and chilli sauce
and simmer slowly until rice is
cooked. Add mussels and heat for
another 2 minutes. Season to taste.

Tuna curry
Serves 4

1 tablespoon margarine
1 onion, chopped
1 tablespoon curry powder
1 x 410 g can tomatoes,
   chopped
a little water
1 tablespoon seedless raisins
1 x 210 g can tuna
salt and pepper to taste
lemon juice

Melt the margarine and fry onion
until soft. Add curry powder and
fry for another 2 minutes. Add
tomatoes, water, raisins and tuna.
Season and simmer gently for
15 minutes. Finish with a dash
of lemon juice.

Kedgeree
Serves 4

2 tablespoons margarine
2 cups cooked, deboned and
   flaked fish
2 cups cooked rice
salt and pepper to taste
2 hard-boiled eggs, sliced

Melt margarine and add fish,
stirring constantly. Add rice,
season well and arrange egg
slices on top before serving.

Tuna balls
Serves 4

1 small onion, chopped
4 tablespoons margarine
1 slice white bread, crusts
  removed and bread crumbled
½ cup milk
salt and black pepper to taste
pinch of grated nutmeg
2 x 210 g cans tuna, flaked
1 egg, beaten
plain (cake) flour
oil for frying

Fry onion in margarine until golden. Soak the breadcrumbs in milk for about 5 minutes then drain. Add salt, pepper, nutmeg, onion, tuna and egg. Shape mixture into balls and roll in flour. Fry tuna balls in hot oil until brown on all sides.

Fish cakes
Serves 2

1 x 120 g can sardines
1 tablespoon margarine
1 teaspoon dried parsley
1 egg, beaten
1 cup mashed potato
salt and pepper to taste

COATING
1 egg, beaten
fine white breadcrumbs
oil for frying

Mix all fish cake ingredients together, and shape into balls. Roll balls in the egg and then in the breadcrumbs. Fry in oil until brown on all sides. For an easy tartare sauce to serve with the fish cakes, simply open a bottle of sandwich spread.

Fish stew
Serves 6

1 onion, chopped
3 cups diced raw fish
2 tablespoons margarine
2 cups white wine
2 cups sliced mushrooms
salt and pepper to taste
1 teaspoon dried parsley
½ cup cream
cornflour

Lightly fry the onion and fish in margarine until just starting to brown. Add wine, mushrooms, seasoning and parsley and bring to the boil. Simmer gently for about 8 minutes, or until fish is cooked. Add cream and heat through. Bind to a creamy consistency with cornflour that has been blended with a little water.

Fish and potato bake
Serves 6

2 x 210 g cans fish (tuna,
  salmon, sardines), flaked
1 cup mashed potato
1 onion, chopped
2 tomatoes, sliced
1 cup thin white sauce
  (see page 93)
½ cup grated Cheddar cheese

Spoon half the fish into a greased,
fireproof dish. Spoon half the
mashed potato over and then
half the onion, tomato and white
sauce. Repeat layers, ending with
a layer of white sauce. Sprinkle
with cheese. Put a lid on the dish
(or cover with aluminium foil)
and place on a grid over very low
heat (scrape a few coals to one
side under the grid) until dish
is warmed through and cheese
has melted.

Sardines with rice
Serves 4–6

1 x 60 g packet chicken
  noodle soup
2 cups boiling water
½ cup rice, uncooked
1 x 425 g can sardines in
  tomato sauce
1 egg, beaten
2 teaspoons vinegar
1 onion, chopped
1 tomato, chopped
pinch of dried thyme
½ cup grated Cheddar cheese

Stir soup into boiling water and
simmer for 6 minutes. Cook rice
in a separate saucepan until soft.
Remove bones from fish and mix
the fish, soup, rice and remaining
ingredients, except the cheese,
together. Spoon into a greased,
fireproof dish and sprinkle with
cheese. Cover with a lid or foil and
place dish on a grid over low heat
until food is warmed through.

Curried salmon
Serves 2

1 tablespoon margarine
1 small onion, chopped
2 teaspoons curry powder
2 teaspoons plain (cake) flour
½ cup chicken stock
1 tablespoon vinegar
1 tablespoon chutney
1 x 210 g can pink salmon

Melt the margarine, add the onion
and fry until golden. Stir in the
curry powder, cook for about
3 minutes, then add the flour
and continue cooking for another
2 minutes. Remove from heat
and gradually pour in the stock,
stirring constantly. Return to heat
and bring to the boil. Reduce
heat and add vinegar and chutney.
Leave to simmer for 10 minutes.
Add the salmon and heat through,
but do not allow to boil or the fish
to break up.

Kipper pie
Serves 2

1 x 200 g can kipper fillets in
   vegetable oil
boiling water
½ packet instant mashed
   potato
salt and black pepper to taste
1 teaspoon margarine

Heat kippers in the can according
to the instructions on the label.
Add enough boiling water to
instant potatoes to form soft
mash. Season with salt and
pepper and stir in margarine.
Place kippers in a flat-bottomed
dish and spoon mash on top.
Draw decorative patterns in the
mash with a fork. If desired, the
top of the dish may be browned
slightly by heating a metal plate
on a grid over very hot coals and
then placing the warm plate over
the dish (take care not to get ash
or dirt into the food).

Chicken

Chicken in foil
Serves 6

1 chicken, cut into portions
1 onion, peeled and sliced
3 potatoes, peeled and sliced
2 tomatoes, sliced
1 cup chopped mushrooms
1 green pepper, seeded and
  sliced
2 teaspoons salt
pepper to taste
3 tablespoons margarine

Place each chicken portion on a piece of heavy duty foil (shiny side facing chicken). Divide vegetables between the portions and sprinkle with salt and pepper. Put a little margarine on top of each portion and fold foil to form a parcel, leaving space for the air to expand. Place on a grid over hot coals for about 40 minutes, or until chicken is cooked, turning the parcels every now and then.

Chicken potjie 1
Serves 6–8

10 chicken thighs
1 tablespoon oil
2 onions, sliced
1 clove garlic, crushed
6 carrots, peeled and sliced
6 sweet potatoes, peeled and
  sliced
2 stalks celery, chopped
  (if available)
1 cup dried peaches
2 teaspoons salt
2 cups dry white wine
1 cinnamon stick
2 bay leaves

Fry chicken in oil until golden-brown. Add onion and garlic and fry for a few more minutes until onion is soft. Add carrots, sweet potatoes, celery, peaches and salt. Add wine, cinnamon and bay leaves, cover pot and simmer gently for about 1 hour. Remove cinnamon stick and bay leaves before serving on a bed of rice.

Chicken potjie 2
Serves 6

1 chicken, cut into portions
salt and pepper to taste
1 teaspoon dried thyme
2 onions, sliced
2 sweet potatoes, peeled and
  sliced
1 cup dried peaches
1½ cups water

SAUCE
1 cup tomato sauce
½ cup oil
2 tablespoons vinegar
1 tablespoon Worcestershire
  sauce
2 teaspoons paprika
1 teaspoon crushed garlic
1 teaspoon salt
1 teaspoon cayenne pepper
4 drops Tabasco® sauce

Season chicken with salt, pepper
and thyme. Pack chicken, onions,
sweet potatoes and peaches in
layers in a large cast-iron pot,
and pour water over. Cover and
simmer for 30 minutes.
　Mix all the ingredients for the
sauce and add to the chicken.
Simmer for another 1½ hours.

Chicken kebabs 1
Serves 2

MARINADE
2 tablespoons brown sugar
1 tablespoon Worcestershire
  sauce
2 tablespoons lemon juice
pinch of salt

2 chicken breast fillets, diced
8 small onions, peeled but
  preferably with ends intact
  (or larger onions, quartered)
3 firm bananas, peeled and
  quartered
6 rashers bacon, halved
1 green pepper, seeded and cut
  into pieces the same size as
  the onions

Mix ingredients for marinade and
marinate chicken for 4 hours.
　Simmer onions in boiling water
for 5 minutes. Drain chicken and
set marinade aside. Wrap each
piece of banana in bacon and dip
into marinade. Alternate chicken,
banana, onion and green pepper
on four kebab skewers and brush
with marinade. Place on a grill
over medium-hot coals for about
20 minutes, turning and basting
the kebabs frequently with left-
over marinade.

Chicken kebabs 2
Serves 4

4 chicken breast fillets
8 small onions, peeled but
  preferably with ends intact
  (or larger onions, quartered)
1 green pepper, seeded and cut
  into pieces the same size as
  the onions
8 dried apricots, soaked in a
  little water
8 mushrooms
½ teaspoon ground allspice
4 tablespoons margarine,
  melted

Cut chicken into cubes. Thread
onto skewers with onions, green
pepper, apricots and mushrooms.
Grill over medium-hot coals for
about 20 minutes, or until chicken
is done, basting all the time with a
mixture of allspice and margarine.

HANDY HINT
Crushed breakfast cornflakes can
be used as a coating on chicken
portions instead of breadcrumbs.

Chicken stuffing
For 1 chicken

1 onion, finely chopped
2 tablespoons margarine
2 cups very finely chopped ham
3 tablespoons white
  breadcrumbs
1 teaspoon dried parsley
½ teaspoon dried tarragon
grated rind and juice of
  ½ lemon
1 egg, beaten
salt and pepper to taste

Fry the onion in margarine until
soft. Cool, then mix with ham,
breadcrumbs, herbs and lemon
rind. Bind with lemon juice and
egg, then add seasoning. Stuff
chicken, wrap in a double layer
of aluminium foil, and bake in
medium-hot coals for about
1 hour, or until chicken is cooked.

Fruit stuffing
For 1 chicken

2 onions, chopped
2 tablespoons margarine
1 x 410 g can apricots or
  pineapple, drained and
  chopped
2 cups cooked rice
1 egg, beaten
pinch of salt
1 teaspoon dried parsley

Fry onions in margarine until soft. Remove from heat and allow to cool. Add remaining ingredients and mix well before stuffing the chicken with the mixture.

Bread stuffing
For 1 chicken

1½ tablespoons margarine
1 tablespoon chopped onion
2 cups white breadcrumbs
1 teaspoon salt
¼ teaspoon pepper
½ teaspoon dried thyme
½ teaspoon celery salt
½ teaspoon dried parsley
½ cup milk

Melt margarine and fry onion until light brown. Add remaining ingredients and mix well. Stuff chicken with mixture.

Chicken casserole
Serves 4–6

1 x 60 g packet mushroom soup
1½ cups water
1 chicken, cooked, deboned and
  cut into small pieces
1 cup crushed potato crisps
1 cup cooked peas
1 cup grated Cheddar cheese

Prepare soup according to instructions on the packet and cook until ready. Pack layers of the chicken, potato crisps, peas and cheese in a greased, fireproof pot. Pour soup over and sprinkle with left-over potato crisps from packet. Cover and place on a grid over low heat. Put a few hot coals on top of the lid and bake for about 20 minutes.

Chicken with asparagus sauce
Serves 4

4 chicken breast fillets
1 tablespoon plain (cake) flour,
  seasoned with salt and pepper
2 tablespoons margarine
1 onion, finely chopped
1 x 410 g can whole
  asparagus spears, drained
  (reserve liquid)
¼ cup dry white wine
salt and black pepper to taste
¼ cup milk, blended with
  2 teaspoons cornflour
1 tablespoon grated Parmesan
  cheese (optional)

Coat chicken with seasoned flour
and fry in margarine until golden-
brown. Remove and set aside. Fry
onion until light brown. Keep
8 asparagus pieces aside. Add
remaining asparagus and liquid,
wine and seasoning to onions,
return chicken to pan and simmer
for 20 minutes, or until chicken
is cooked. Remove chicken to a
heated bowl and keep warm. With
a fork or potato masher, mash
asparagus and onion, then thicken
sauce with milk and cornflour
mixture. Add Parmesan cheese and
adjust seasoning. Pour sauce over
chicken and garnish with reserved
asparagus spears.

Chicken with peaches
Serves 6

1 chicken, cut into portions
salt and pepper to taste
oil for frying
1 onion, chopped
1 x 410 g can peach slices
1 cup orange juice
½ cup apple juice
2 tablespoons sugar
½ teaspoon mustard powder
½ teaspoon ground ginger

Season chicken with salt and
pepper and brown in the oil. Add
the onion and fry until soft. Mix
remaining ingredients and add to
chicken. Simmer gently over very
low heat for 1 hour.

Broccoli chicken
Serves 6

2 cups broccoli, cooked
1 chicken, cooked and deboned
1 x 410 g can cream of
  mushroom soup
2 teaspoons curry powder
¼ cup mayonnaise
1 tablespoon lemon juice
  (optional)
salt and pepper to taste
2 cups grated Cheddar cheese

Mix all the ingredients together,
except the cheese. Spoon into a
fireproof dish and sprinkle with
cheese. Cover with a lid or foil
and place on a grid over low coals
for about 20 minutes, or until
heated through.

Chicken stew
Serves 6–8

1 chicken, cut into small
  portions
1 x 60 g packet mushroom soup
1 cup macaroni
4 tablespoons margarine
2 onions, chopped
4 tomatoes, chopped
½ cup plain (cake) flour
2 cups water

Simmer chicken for approximately
45 minutes, or until tender, in
lightly salted water. Add soup
powder (and more water if
necessary to make about 2 cups).
Boil for 10 minutes. In a separate
saucepan, cook macaroni in plenty
of salted water until soft, then
drain. In a separate pan, melt
margarine, add onions and sauté
until brown. Add tomatoes and
sauté for a further 4 minutes.
Mix flour with water and stir into
tomato mixture. Add soup, chicken
and macaroni and heat through.

Chicken in red wine
Serves 6

4 tablespoons margarine
1 chicken, cut into portions
1 onion, chopped
1 clove garlic, crushed
¼ cup plain (cake) flour
1 teaspoon tomato paste
½ cup red wine
1 cup chicken stock
½ teaspoon dried mixed herbs
½ teaspoon salt
¼ teaspoon black pepper
1 cup sliced mushrooms
2 tomatoes, chopped
1 tablespoon cornflour, blended
  with a little water

Melt margarine in a pan, brown
chicken on both sides, drain on
paper towel and place in a separate
saucepan. Drain off excess fat,
leaving about 2 tablespoons in the
pan. Fry onion and garlic until
soft, then add flour, tomato paste,
wine, stock, herbs and seasoning.
Bring to the boil, stirring, then
add mushrooms and tomatoes.
Pour over chicken, cover and
place on a grid over low to
medium-hot coals to simmer
for about 1½ hours. Thicken
sauce with blended cornflour and
simmer for another 5 minutes.

Hot chicken legs
Serves 4

2 teaspoons Worcestershire
  sauce
½ cup dry sherry
1 tablespoon vinegar
2 teaspoons prepared English
  mustard
salt and pepper to taste
4 chicken joints or 8 drumsticks
¼ cup oil

Mix the Worcestershire sauce,
sherry, vinegar, mustard and
seasoning in a small bowl. Make
a few cuts in the chicken and
place in a shallow dish. Pour the
sherry mixture over and leave
to marinate for at least 1 hour,
turning from time to time. Cook
the chicken over medium-hot
coals for 15 minutes on each side,
basting alternately with the sherry
mixture and oil.

Hungarian chicken
Serves 4–6

2 onions, thinly sliced
2 cloves garlic, crushed
4 tablespoons margarine
2 tablespoons oil
1½ teaspoons paprika
6 chicken portions, skinned
1½ cups chicken stock
2 tomatoes, chopped
1 tablespoon sherry
½ cup plain yoghurt
1 tablespoon cornflour
1 green pepper, seeded
  and sliced

Fry onions and garlic in
2 tablespoons each margarine
and oil until brown. Add paprika
and mix well. Add chicken and
fry for 5 minutes, turning portions
until coated with paprika mixture.
Cover and sauté for 20 minutes.
Add stock and tomatoes and
simmer for 40 minutes, or until
chicken is tender. Remove chicken
to a bowl and keep warm. Reduce
sauce over high heat to about
1 cup, and stir in sherry. Mix
yoghurt and cornflour together
and add to sauce. Bring to the
boil, then pour over chicken.
Sauté green pepper in remaining
margarine and use to garnish
chicken. Serve with noodles.

Chicken and rice cakes
Serves 4

1 cup cooked rice
½ cup Béchamel sauce
  (see page 93)
½ cup chopped nuts
2 cups cooked, chopped chicken
½ cup sultanas
1 teaspoon curry powder
2 egg yolks
salt and pepper to taste
a little plain (cake) flour
1 egg, beaten
breadcrumbs for coating
oil for deep-frying

Mix the rice, sauce, nuts, chicken,
sultanas, curry powder and egg
yolks. Season, then form into eight
cakes. Chill for 3 hours in a cooler
box or refrigerator. Coat the cakes
in flour, dip into egg and coat
with breadcrumbs, taking care to
cover the cakes completely. Heat
the oil for deep-frying and add the
cakes one or two at a time. Cook
until crisp and golden. Drain on
absorbent paper towel.

Stir-fried chicken
Serves 4

2 tablespoons oil
3 cups raw, deboned chicken,
  cut into strips
salt and pepper to taste
2 carrots, cut into strips
1 tablespoon grated lemon rind
1 cup sliced mushrooms
2 tablespoons flaked almonds
1 bunch spring onions, sliced
  lengthways (if not available,
  onions cut into rings)

Heat the oil in a large pan and add
the chicken and seasoning. Stir-fry
until the meat is lightly browned,
then add the carrots and lemon
rind and continue to fry for a few
minutes. Stir in the mushrooms
and fry for a few seconds. (The
cooked vegetables should still be
crisp.) Transfer the stir-fry to a
serving bowl. Quickly toss the
almonds in the fat remaining
in the pan until they are lightly
browned, then stir in the onions.
(If using spring onions, stir-fry
for a few seconds. If using onion,
stir-fry until golden.) Spoon this
mixture over the chicken and serve
immediately.

Pineapple chicken
Serves 4

4 chicken pieces
4 tablespoons oil
1 green pepper, seeded and
  chopped
2 stalks celery, chopped
  (if available)
1 onion, chopped
1 x 198 g can pineapple slices,
  drained (reserve syrup)
1 tablespoon each soy sauce,
  lemon juice and tomato purée
salt and pepper to taste

Fry chicken in oil until golden.
Add green pepper, celery and
onion and sauté gently until
softened. Add pineapple syrup,
soy sauce, lemon juice, tomato
purée and seasoning. Cover
and simmer gently for about
30 minutes or until chicken is
cooked. Arrange pineapple slices
on top of chicken and put back on
heat for 5 minutes before serving.

Sweet-and-sour chicken
Serves 4–6

4 tablespoons margarine
1 onion, chopped
1 green pepper, seeded and
  chopped
2 teaspoons curry powder
½ teaspoon paprika
1½ tablespoons plain
  (cake) flour
½ cup chicken stock
1 cup chopped fresh pineapple
  (or canned crushed pineapple)
1 tablespoon vinegar
2 teaspoons sugar
salt and pepper to taste
1 chicken, cut into portions

Melt margarine and fry onion, green pepper, curry powder and paprika for 5 minutes. Add flour and stir in stock and remaining ingredients, except chicken. Bring to the boil, stirring. Add chicken and simmer for about 1 hour or more until chicken is cooked.

Honey chicken
Serves 4

4 tablespoons margarine
1 onion, thinly sliced
4 chicken portions, skinned
2 tablespoons plain (cake) flour

SAUCE
6 tablespoons honey
2 tablespoons lemon juice
½ teaspoon dried rosemary
juice of 1 orange
¼ cup water
salt and black pepper to taste
1 tablespoon cornflour, blended
  with a little water

Melt margarine and fry onion. Coat chicken pieces in flour, then brown.

Combine honey, lemon juice, rosemary, orange juice, water and seasoning in a separate saucepan and bring to the boil, stirring frequently. Add chicken and onion and simmer for about 1 hour, or until chicken is cooked.

Remove chicken and keep warm. Thicken sauce over low heat with blended cornflour. Replace chicken and serve.

Meat

Mutton curry
Serves 6–8

salt and pepper to taste
2 kg mutton chops
4 tablespoons oil
2 onions, chopped
1 x 250 g packet bacon, cut
    into small pieces
3 potatoes, peeled and diced
1 cup rice, uncooked
1 cup dried apricots
1 cup water
1 cup chutney
2 tablespoons curry powder
1 teaspoon turmeric
½ teaspoon ground coriander
½ teaspoon grated nutmeg
1 x 410 g can corn kernels,
    drained
1 x 410 g can peas, drained

Sprinkle salt and pepper over meat
and fry in oil until brown. Remove
from potjie and fry onions and
bacon in the remaining fat. Pack
meat, potatoes, rice and apricots
in layers on top of the onions and
bacon. Add water, cover and
simmer for 1 hour, adding more
water if necessary. Mix chutney,
curry powder, turmeric, coriander
and nutmeg and stir into the meat
together with the corn kernels
and peas. Cover again and simmer
slowly for another 30 minutes.

Minced meat potjie
Serves 6

1 onion, chopped
1 clove garlic, crushed
2 tablespoons oil
1 kg minced meat
2 tablespoons curry powder
1 meat stock cube dissolved in
    ½ cup hot water
2 tablespoons apricot jam
½ tablespoon salt
pepper to taste
1 x 410 g can whole tomatoes,
    drained and chopped
½ cup sultanas
4 bananas, sliced

Fry onion and garlic in oil until
brown. Add meat and curry
powder and brown. Add meat
extract, jam, seasoning, tomatoes
and sultanas and simmer for about
30 minutes over very low heat.
Add bananas just before serving.

HANDY HINT

Black cast-iron casserole pots
(potjies) are sturdy and can be used
over the fire or on gas. They are also
ideal for baking food in the ground
(see page 6, Dutch oven).

Orange-glazed cutlets
Serves 4

8 lamb chops

GLAZE
grated rind and juice of
  1 large orange
2 tablespoons oil
1 clove garlic, crushed
salt and pepper to taste
dash of Worcestershire sauce
1 tablespoon sugar

Mix the orange rind and juice
with oil, garlic, seasoning,
Worcestershire sauce and sugar.
  Brush the lamb generously
with the mixture and cook over
medium-hot coals for about
20 minutes, basting frequently
with the glaze and turning
the meat from time to time.

Biltong potjie 1
Serves 4

8 cups water
2 teaspoons salt
2 cups mealie meal
2 cups finely sliced biltong
grated cheese

Bring salted water to the boil and
add mealie meal slowly, stirring all
the time. Steam for 30–45 minutes
over low heat. Add biltong and
mix well. Sprinkle with cheese and
cover dish until cheese has melted.

Biltong potjie 2
Serves 4

1 x 200 g packet Spanish rice
1 cup grated Cheddar cheese
1 cup finely sliced biltong
1 tablespoon lemon juice or
  vinegar (optional)

Cook the rice according to the
instructions on the packet. When
the rice is cooked, drain, then add
cheese, biltong and lemon juice
and stir until cheese has melted.
Serve with a tomato salad.

Wiener marzetti
Serves 4–6

1 x 68 g packet onion soup
4 cups tomato juice
1 cup noodles, uncooked
1 x 510 g can Wiener sausages
½ cup grated Cheddar cheese

Blend soup powder with tomato
juice, then heat. Add noodles,
bring to the boil and simmer for
about 15 minutes until noodles are
soft. Cut sausages in half crosswise
and add to pot. Simmer, covered,
for 5 minutes. Sprinkle with cheese
before serving.

Safari casserole
Serves 4

1 x 95 g packet mixed
  dehydrated vegetables
1 teaspoon dried mixed herbs
salt and pepper to taste
1 x 340 g can corned beef, cut
  into small pieces

Prepare vegetables according to
the haybox cooking method (see
page 7). Add herbs, seasoning and
beef and cook slowly over low heat
for 5–10 minutes. Serve with rice
or instant mashed potato.

Lamb chops in foil
Serves 4–6

8 lamb chops
1 tablespoon oil
2 onions, finely chopped
3 tomatoes, chopped
2 tablespoons chutney
1 teaspoon salt
black pepper to taste

Quickly brown chops on both
sides over hot coals. Place each
chop on a piece of aluminium
foil. Heat oil and fry onions
until light brown. Add tomatoes,
chutney and seasoning and simmer
for 5 minutes. Spoon a little of the
mixture onto each chop, fold foil
to close securely and place over
hot coals for about 30 minutes
or until meat is done.

Tomato stew
Serves 6

2 onions, chopped
1 kg mutton rib
2 tablespoons fruit chutney
1 large can tomato purée
1 bay leaf
1 teaspoon dried thyme
1 teaspoon dried rosemary
salt and pepper to taste
1 x 410 g can peas, drained
4 large potatoes, peeled and
  quartered

Fry the onions and mutton until
brown. Add all other ingredients,
except the peas and potatoes, and
simmer over medium heat for
about 1½ hours or until the meat
is cooked. Add the potatoes and
cook for 15–20 minutes until the
potatoes are soft. Add the peas
10 minutes before serving to
heat through.

Corned beef fritters
Serves 2

1 x 340 g can corned beef
batter for fritters (see page 116)
oil for frying

Cut corned beef into thick slices.
Prepare batter. Dip slices of meat
in the batter and fry in oil until
both sides are brown and crisp.

Beef and mushroom goulash
Serves 8

3 onions, chopped
4 tablespoons oil
600 g cubed beef
flour
3 cups red wine
2 slices each lemon and
  orange rind
1 bay leaf
salt and pepper to taste
4 cups sliced mushrooms

Fry onions in oil until light brown.
Add meat and fry for a few minutes
more. Sprinkle flour over meat and
onion and fry another 5 minutes.
Add remaining ingredients, except
mushrooms, and simmer for 1 hour,
or until meat is tender. Add the
mushrooms 10 minutes before the
end of the cooking time.

Ember chops
Serves 4–6

8 lamb chops
margarine
1 teaspoon dried mixed herbs
salt and pepper to taste

Wrap chops in heavy duty foil
with margarine, herbs and
seasoning. Make sure the chops
are wrapped securely, then
cook them in the embers for
at least 30 minutes, turning
the parcels frequently.

Pork chops in foil
Serves 4–6

6 pork chops
5 teaspoons margarine
1 sweet potato, peeled and
  sliced
2 apples, peeled, cored and
  sliced
1 teaspoon salt
pepper to taste
5 teaspoons sugar

Brown chops quickly on both
sides over the coals. Place each
one on a square of foil (shiny
side facing chops) that has been
greased with margarine. Divide
sweet potato and apple slices
between the parcels and season.
Put a little margarine on each
and sprinkle with sugar. Fold foil
to close securely and place on
a grid over hot coals for about
30 minutes or until meat is cooked
and sweet potatoes are soft.

HANDY HINT
When baking food or when keeping
it warm, place the shiny side of the
foil to the inside (to reflect the heat
to the inside). To keep food cool,
place the shiny side to the outside
(to reflect the heat to the outside).

Pork chops Mediterranean
Serves 6

1 teaspoon salt
1 teaspoon black pepper
6 pork chops
3 tablespoons oil
2 cloves garlic, crushed
1 teaspoon dried basil
1 teaspoon dried thyme
1 bay leaf
¼ cup dry red wine
1 x 410 g can whole tomatoes, drained and chopped
1 tablespoon tomato purée
3 tablespoons margarine
3 green peppers, seeded and chopped
1 onion, sliced
1 cup sliced mushrooms
4½ teaspoons cornflour

Rub the salt and pepper into the pork chops. Heat oil in a heavy-based pan, add the chops and brown for 3 minutes on each side. Add the garlic, basil, thyme and bay leaf. Pour in the wine and bring to the boil, then stir in the tomatoes and tomato purée. Cover pan and simmer for 40 minutes, turning the chops from time to time. In a separate pan, melt the margarine and add the green peppers and onion. Cook for 5–10 minutes, stirring occasionally. Add the mushrooms and cook for a further 3 minutes. Add vegetables to meat when pork is cooked and simmer, uncovered, for 15 minutes. Remove pork from pan and thicken sauce with cornflour (blended with a little water). Pour sauce over chops just before serving.

Cheesy steaks
Serves 4

2 tablespoons prepared English mustard
1 tablespoon oil
1 tablespoon lemon juice
4 steaks
½ teaspoon dried mixed herbs
4 slices Cheddar cheese

Mix mustard, oil and lemon juice. Grill steaks for about 6 minutes on one side (or longer if meat is preferred well-done) over hot coals. Turn, then smear half the mustard mixture on the cooked side. Grill for another 6 minutes, turn and smear the rest of the mustard mixture on the other side. Sprinkle with herbs and top each steak with a slice of cheese. Serve immediately.

Sweet-and-sour meatballs
Serves 4

450 g minced beef
1 onion, grated
½ teaspoon dried mixed herbs
salt and pepper to taste
2 tablespoons oil

SAUCE
1 carrot, peeled and cut into
  thin strips
1½ cups beef stock
4 tablespoons vinegar
5 tablespoons sugar
4 teaspoons cornflour
1 teaspoon soy sauce

Mix the minced beef, onion, herbs and seasoning. Form into small balls and fry in oil for about 15 minutes. Drain on absorbent paper towel.

Cook the carrot, stock, vinegar and sugar in a saucepan for 5 minutes. Blend the cornflour with the soy sauce and a little water and add to the sauce. Simmer for 5 minutes before pouring sauce over the meatballs. Serve.

Hungarian goulash
Serves 4

1 green pepper, seeded and
  sliced
1 onion, chopped
1 tablespoon oil
4 potatoes, peeled and halved
1 x 410 g can tomatoes
2 teaspoons paprika
1 teaspoon sugar
salt and pepper to taste
1 x 400 g can braised steak
2 teaspoons cornflour

Fry green pepper and onion in oil for about 4 minutes. Add potatoes to the pan with tomatoes and stir in the paprika, sugar and seasoning. Simmer gently for about 10 minutes. Add braised steak and simmer for another 10 minutes or until the potatoes are tender. If necessary, thicken with cornflour (which has been blended with a little water).

Goulash
Serves 4

1 kg stewing steak
seasoned flour
2 onions
1 green pepper
3 tablespoons oil
2 tablespoons tomato purée
salt and pepper to taste
pinch of grated nutmeg
4 tablespoons plain (cake) flour
1 cup beef stock
2 tomatoes, chopped
2 teaspoons paprika

Cut the steak into small cubes and dip them in seasoned flour. Chop the onions and green pepper and fry in oil, then add the meat and fry lightly on all sides. Stir in the tomato purée, seasonings and flour. Add the stock and tomatoes. Simmer gently for 1 hour, then add paprika and cook for another 20 minutes.

Boerewors dish
Serves 6

500 g boerewors, grilled or fried
until brown and cooked
1 tablespoon oil
1 onion, sliced
1 clove garlic, crushed
1 green pepper, seeded and
sliced
1 meat stock cube dissolved in
½ cup hot water
1 x 410 g can baked beans in
tomato sauce
salt and pepper to taste

Cut boerewors into small pieces. Heat oil and fry onion, garlic and green pepper until onion is translucent. Add meat extract and simmer for a few minutes. Add boerewors, beans and seasoning, and heat through before serving.

Hotch potch
Serves 4

1 x 410 g can baked beans in
tomato sauce
1 medium can macaroni and
cheese sauce
1 x 280 g can luncheon meat
margarine

Heat the baked beans and macaroni. Cut the meat into thick slices and fry in margarine until golden-brown. Spoon macaroni and beans over meat and serve with bread.

Shepherd's pie
Serves 4–6

1 large onion, chopped
1 x 405 g can mushrooms,
  chopped
2 tablespoons oil
1 x 400 g can minced beef
salt and pepper to taste
1 x 112 g packet instant
  mashed potato
margarine
milk

Fry onion and mushrooms in oil
until soft. Stir in the minced beef
and seasoning. Prepare the instant
mashed potato according to the
instructions on the packet, adding
a little margarine and milk to
make it creamier. Spoon the meat
mixture into a dish and spread
potato over the top. If you want
to brown the potato topping,
carefully place a heated metal sheet
over the dish until the potatoes are
grilled (be careful not to get ash or
dirt into the dish).

> HANDY HINT
> Pack soya mince for emergencies
> (when you don't have enough food,
> or floods prevent you from getting
> to the next shop) as it is lightweight,
> filling and economical.

Sweet-and-sour sausages
Serves 4

1 large can pork sausages
1 tablespoon margarine
1 onion, chopped
1 green pepper, seeded and
  chopped
1 tablespoon cornflour, blended
  with a little water
1 x 440 g can pineapple pieces,
  drained (reserve syrup)
2 tablespoons brown sugar
  or honey
2 tablespoons vinegar
salt and pepper to taste

Fry the sausages in margarine until
brown. Remove from pan and fry
the onion and green pepper until
soft. Stir in cornflour and add
pineapple syrup. Simmer gently
for 3 minutes. Add remaining
ingredients and simmer for
30 minutes. If sauce becomes
too thick, add a little water.
Add sausages and heat through
before serving.

Wiener sausages with potatoes
Serves 4–6

8–12 Wiener sausages
prepared mustard
2 cups mashed potato
  (instant mashed potato may
  also be used)
½ cup grated Cheddar cheese

Place sausages in freshly boiled
water for about 10 minutes to
warm through. Cut each one
lengthways, but not right through.
Smear insides with mustard. Mix
potatoes and cheese and heap
mixture between sausage halves.
Serve immediately.

Frankfurter stew
Serves 4

1 onion, sliced into rings
1 green pepper, seeded and
  chopped
1 tablespoon margarine
8 Frankfurter sausages,
  quartered
1 x 410 g can condensed
  tomato soup, mixed with
  a little milk
salt and pepper to taste
1 teaspoon brown sugar
1 teaspoon Worcestershire sauce
½ lemon, thinly sliced

Fry the onion rings and green
pepper in margarine. Add the
Frankfurters and brown slightly.
Pour in the soup and leave to
simmer for 5 minutes. Add the
seasoning, sugar, Worcestershire
sauce and lemon slices and
simmer for a further 3 minutes.
Serve with bread.

Chilli con carne
Serves 4

1 kg minced beef
1 large onion, finely chopped
oil for frying
1 green pepper, seeded and
  chopped
1 x 410 g can diced tomatoes
1 teaspoon salt
2 teaspoons chilli powder
1 x 410 g can baked beans in
  tomato sauce
1 teaspoon dried origanum
1 clove garlic, crushed
½ cup water

Brown the meat and onions
in a little oil. Add remaining
ingredients and cook for
20 minutes. Serve with rice
or fresh bread.

Pot roast
Serves 8

4 tablespoons oil
1.5 kg topside roast
boiling water

SAUCE
1 teaspoon salt
pinch of pepper
1 x 225 g can tomato purée (or
  2 fresh tomatoes, chopped)
1 beef stock cube dissolved
  in ½ cup boiling water
1 tablespoon Worcestershire
  sauce
1 onion, chopped
½ cup dry red wine

Heat oil in a heavy-based cast-iron
saucepan. Brown meat on all
sides. Mix all sauce ingredients
together and set aside. Pour
enough boiling water over the
meat just to cover it and simmer
slowly until all the water has
evaporated, or until meat is tender
when pierced with a long fork.
Add sauce to meat and cook for
about 30 minutes, or until liquid
starts to reduce and thicken.

Vegetables
(side dishes)

Potato casserole
Serves 8–10

4 onions, sliced
4 tablespoons margarine
8 potatoes, cooked and diced
6 rashers bacon, cut into small
   pieces and fried until crisp
1 cup milk
½ cup chutney
3 eggs, beaten
1 teaspoon dried parsley
¼ teaspoon grated nutmeg
1 teaspoon salt
¼ teaspoon pepper
½ cup grated Cheddar cheese

Fry onions in margarine until
golden-brown. Mix with potatoes
and bacon and place in a greased,
fireproof dish. Whisk milk,
chutney, eggs, parsley, nutmeg
and seasoning and pour over the
potatoes. Sprinkle with cheese.
Cover with lid and place on a
grid over medium-low coals. Place
a few coals on top of the lid and
bake for about 1 hour, or until
milk mixture has set.

Stuffed baked potatoes

Wrap clean, scrubbed potatoes
(one per person) in foil (shiny
side facing in). Place in hot coals
for about 45 minutes, or until
potatoes are soft. Unwrap, cut a
piece off the top of each potato
and scoop out some of the flesh.

Fill with one of the following:
❖ Cream cheese and chives
❖ Salmon or tuna, mixed with
  mayonnaise
❖ Crisp-fried bacon cubes
❖ Fried onion rings
❖ Cottage cheese and ham
❖ Mussels and prawns
❖ Salami and gherkins
❖ Sour cream
❖ Freshly squeezed lemon juice
  and black pepper

> **HANDY HINT**
> To make sour cream (to serve with
> baked potatoes), add 1 tablespoon
> lemon juice to 1 cup long-life
> cream and mix well.

Curry potatoes
Serves 4

4 potatoes, cooked and diced

SAUCE
1 onion, sliced
2 tablespoons margarine
salt and pepper to taste
1 tablespoon curry powder
1 tablespoon sugar
1 tablespoon flour
1 beef stock cube, dissolved in
   1 cup boiling water
1 tablespoon vinegar

Fry onion in margarine until light brown. Mix in dry ingredients. Add beef stock and vinegar and simmer, stirring, until sauce has thickened.

Pour sauce over potatoes, mix lightly and serve.

Mock roast potatoes

Peel potatoes and cut them into quarters. Try to keep the cut potatoes the same size to ensure even cooking. Heat enough oil for deep-frying in a saucepan and fry potatoes in batches until cooked and brown. If you prepare this for more than two people, do not fry all the potatoes at once, as they will not crisp and will become soggy. Drain potatoes on absorbent paper towel and add salt to taste. Allow at least one potato per person.

Potatoes in foil
Serves 4

3 large potatoes, peeled and
   diced
1 teaspoon salt
½ teaspoon pepper
4 rashers bacon, cut into small
   pieces
1 onion, chopped

Place all ingredients on a piece of foil (shiny side in). Mix lightly and fold foil securely, allowing enough space for air to expand. Place on a grid over hot coals and bake for 30 minutes, or until potatoes are soft.

Potato fritters
Serves 6

3 large potatoes, grated
1 large onion, grated
1 egg
1 teaspoon salt
pinch of pepper
1 tablespoon plain (cake) flour
oil for frying

Mix potatoes and onion with egg, seasoning and flour. Fry tablespoon measures of the mixture in hot oil until brown on both sides.

Potato and cheese fritters
Serves 4

2 large potatoes, peeled and
   grated
4 tablespoons grated cheese
1 egg, beaten
salt and pepper to taste
oil for frying

Mix potatoes, cheese, egg and
seasoning. Heat oil and fry
tablespoon measures of the potato
mixture until brown on both sides.

Potato cakes
Serves 4

1 x 112 g packet instant
   mashed potato
1 egg
salt and pepper to taste
8 rashers bacon, finely chopped
   and fried in a little oil
egg and crumbs for coating
oil for frying

Prepare the potatoes according
to the instructions on the packet,
but make sure the consistency is
not too soft. Mix the potato, egg,
seasoning and bacon together and
form into patties. Dip in egg and
crumbs and fry in a pan until
golden-brown.

Cheese and potato balls
Serves 6

5 potatoes, cooked
1 teaspoon salt
¼ teaspoon cayenne pepper
½ cup grated Cheddar cheese
2 eggs, beaten
½ teaspoon mustard powder
¾ cup plain (cake) flour
1 teaspoon dried parsley
milk for mixing
oil for frying

Mash potatoes and mix with
remaining ingredients, except milk
and oil. Add just enough milk to
make a batter that can be formed
into soft balls. Fry in oil until
brown on all sides.

HANDY HINT
To prevent potatoes from bursting
open when cooking them in their
jackets, prick them with a fork
before boiling.

Potato and onion bake
Serves 6

6 potatoes
2 onions
salt and pepper to taste
1 x 68 g packet brown
  onion soup
2 cups boiling water

Peel potatoes and onions and slice thinly. Pack in layers in a heavy-based saucepan, seasoning with salt and pepper between layers. Mix the soup with the boiling water and pour over dish. Cover with lid and place on a grid over medium-hot coals for about 1 hour, or until potatoes are soft.

Frozen vegetables in foil
Serves 8–10

1 x 1 kg packet frozen
  vegetables (any type)
salt and pepper to taste
1 teaspoon margarine

Place frozen vegetables on a piece of aluminium foil (shiny side facing in). Season vegetables to taste and add margarine. Wrap foil securely, leaving enough space for the expansion of steam. Place parcel on a grid over hot coals, turning occasionally, for about 15 minutes, or until vegetables are tender.

Rice potjie
Serves 4

4 potatoes
1 onion
1 tablespoon margarine
2 cups rice, uncooked

SAUCE
1 x 410 g can diced tomatoes
  (or purée)
2 tablespoons Worcestershire
  sauce
1 teaspoon Tabasco® sauce
2 teaspoons salt

Cut potatoes and onions into rings. Put the margarine in a heavy-based saucepan, and pack potatoes and onions in layers. Add the uncooked rice.
 Mix all the sauce ingredients together and pour over dish.
 Cover and bake over medium-hot coals for about 1 hour, or until potatoes are soft and rice cooked.

VARIATION
Mushrooms or butter beans can be added to the dish before pouring over the sauce. A few sticks of celery, if available, will also add to the flavour.

Rice casserole
Serves 4

3 cups rice, cooked
1 x 425 g can mushroom soup
1 cup grated Cheddar cheese

Put the rice in a heavy-based saucepan. Prepare the soup as directed on the can but use only half the quantity of water indicated. Pour the soup over the rice and cover with cheese. Cover the saucepan with a lid or foil and place it over medium-hot coals until warmed through.

Vegetable risotto
Serves 4

1 tablespoon oil
1 onion, sliced
2 carrots, diced
1 green pepper, seeded and chopped
1 tablespoon yeast extract (Marmite®)
4 cups boiling water
¾ cup rice, uncooked
2 tablespoons tomato purée
¼ cup sultanas
1 x 410 g can peas, drained

Heat oil in a frying pan, add onion and fry gently for about 5 minutes. Add the carrots and cook for a further 5 minutes. Stir in green pepper, yeast extract and boiling water. Add rice, tomato purée and sultanas, then cook for about 20 minutes, stirring occasionally. Check risotto during cooking and add a little extra water if necessary. Stir in peas as soon as rice is cooked and heat through. Serve immediately.

Pumpkin fritters
Serves 6–8

2 cups cooked, mashed
  pumpkin
6 tablespoons plain (cake) flour,
  or enough to thicken batter
2 teaspoons baking powder
pinch of salt
1 egg, beaten
oil for frying
cinnamon sugar

Mix pumpkin, flour, baking
powder and salt. Add egg and
mix well. If the batter is not stiff
enough, add more flour. Heat
oil in a pan and fry tablespoon
measures of pumpkin mixture in
hot oil until brown on both sides.
Serve with cinnamon sugar.

Pumpkin pie 1
Serves 6–8

1½ cups milk
½ cup sugar
¼ teaspoon ground ginger
¼ teaspoon ground allspice
1 teaspoon ground cinnamon
¼ teaspoon salt
1½ cups cooked, mashed
  pumpkin
2 eggs

Add milk, sugar, spices and salt to
pumpkin. Beat the eggs and stir
into the pumpkin mixture. Bake
in a Dutch oven (see page 6) for
1½ hours, or until pie has set.

Pumpkin pie 2
Serves 8–10

2 cups cooked, mashed
  pumpkin (or butternut)
¾ cup evaporated milk or cream
1 cup plain (cake) flour
¾ cup milk
2 teaspoons baking powder
1 teaspoon salt
1 cup sugar
2 eggs, beaten
4 tablespoons melted margarine
cinnamon sugar

Mix all the ingredients together,
except the cinnamon sugar. Pour
into a heavy-based, greased
saucepan and sprinkle cinnamon
sugar over the top. Cover and bake
for 1½ hours, or until pie has set
(see Dutch oven on page 6).

HANDY HINT
As a general rule, brown sugar
gives a better taste to food than
white sugar.

Pumpkin balls in sauce
Serves 8–10

2 cups plain (cake) flour
5 tablespoons sugar
4 teaspoons baking powder
pinch of salt
2 cups cooked, mashed
  pumpkin
2 eggs, beaten
oil for deep-frying

SAUCE
1 cup sugar
1 tablespoon margarine
2 tablespoons custard powder
2 cups milk
1 teaspoon caramel essence

Combine dry ingredients, add pumpkin and mix to a soft dough with the eggs. Deep-fry teaspoon measures of the batter in hot oil. Drain on absorbent paper towel and keep warm in a bowl that has been placed over a saucepan of hot water.

To make the sauce, melt the sugar and margarine over low heat and stir until lightly coloured.

In a separate bowl, mix custard powder to a paste with a little milk. Add remaining milk gradually, stirring all the time. Add to melted sugar mixture. Simmer sauce over low heat until cooked and thickened. Stir in essence. Spoon sauce over pumpkin balls.

This delicious dish can also be served as dessert.

Pumpkin with cinnamon
Serves 10

1 small pumpkin
½ teaspoon salt
½ cup sugar
2 tablespoons margarine
1 teaspoon ground cinnamon

Peel pumpkin and cut into small pieces. Cook in lightly salted water until soft. Drain and mash pumpkin well (this is optional – you may prefer not to mash the pumpkin). Add sugar and margarine to pumpkin and replace over hot coals. Stir continuously and allow sugar to caramelize. Sprinkle cinnamon over pumpkin, mix through and serve hot.

Whole pumpkin in potjie
Serves 8–10

1 round pumpkin which will fit
 into your potjie
4 tablespoons margarine
1 x 410 g can creamed
 sweetcorn
½ cup grated Cheddar cheese
¼ teaspoon grated nutmeg
1 teaspoon dried sage
salt and pepper to taste

Cut off top of pumpkin and
remove seeds inside. Grease inside
of pumpkin and pumpkin lid with
2 tablespoons of margarine. Heat
sweetcorn and add cheese, nutmeg,
sage and seasoning. Spoon into
pumpkin and cover with pumpkin
lid. Place pumpkin in potjie,
cover and put on a grid over
medium-low heat for 2 hours, or
until pumpkin is soft. Remember
to put hot coals on the lid of the
potjie as well. Be careful when
removing the pumpkin from the
potjie because it breaks open easily
once cooked. Serve by cutting the
pumpkin into slices.

Stuffed butternut
Serves 4

1 onion, chopped
1 tablespoon margarine
4 baby marrows (courgettes),
 chopped
1 tomato, chopped
1 green pepper, seeded and
 chopped
1 clove garlic, crushed
1 teaspoon celery salt
pinch of pepper
2 butternuts, halved lengthways
 and pips removed

Fry onion in margarine until soft.
Add all the other ingredients,
except butternuts, and simmer for
about 3 minutes. Spoon mixture
into hollows of butternuts. Wrap
stuffed butternuts individually in
foil (shiny side facing in). Place on
hot coals for 45 minutes, or until
butternuts are tender.

American pumpkin pie
Serves 6

1 cup cooked, mashed pumpkin
2 ripe bananas, mashed
1 x 410 g can evaporated milk
½ cup sugar
2 eggs, beaten
1 teaspoon grated nutmeg
1 tablespoon lemon juice
¼ teaspoon salt

Combine all the ingredients and bake in a Dutch oven (see page 6) for 1½ hours, or until set.

Fried green tomatoes

1 medium-size green tomato
  per person
salt and pepper to taste
white cornmeal or maize meal
bacon dripping

Cut tomato into thick slices, season and coat both sides in cornmeal. Heat enough bacon dripping to coat the base of a pan and fry tomatoes on both sides until lightly browned.

Stuffed tomatoes
Serves 4

4 tomatoes
1 x 285 g can sliced
  mushrooms, drained
1 x 410 g can peas, drained
salt and pepper to taste

Cut a slice off the top of each tomato and scoop out the insides. Mix tomato pulp with remaining ingredients, heat through and spoon back into the tomatoes just before serving.

Stuffed gems
Serves 8–10

6 gem squash, halved and pips
  removed
1 x 410 g can creamed
  sweetcorn

Cook gem squash in lightly salted water until just tender (do not overcook). Drain and keep warm. Just before serving, heat the sweetcorn and spoon into the gem squash. Serve immediately.

Sweet potatoes with orange
Serves 8–10

10 sweet potatoes
4 tablespoons cornflour
2 cups fresh orange juice
½ cup brown sugar
½ teaspoon salt
½ teaspoon grated orange rind
½ cup seedless raisins

Cook sweet potatoes in salted water until slightly soft. Peel and cut into slices. Pack layers into a heavy-based saucepan. Mix cornflour to a smooth paste with a little orange juice. Add remaining orange juice together with the rest of the ingredients. Pour over sweet potatoes. Cover saucepan and simmer over low heat for approximately 30 minutes until sweet potatoes are soft.

VARIATION
Replace the sweet potatoes with pumpkin or carrots.

Stewed sweet potatoes
Serves 4

4 medium sweet potatoes
water
4 tablespoons sugar
  (preferably yellow)
2 tablespoons margarine
dried orange or naartjie peel
pinch of salt
sherry

Peel sweet potatoes and cut into thick slices. Place in a saucepan, add a little water, the sugar, margarine, peel and salt. Stew over medium heat until sweet potatoes are soft. Remove the orange or naartjie peel and add a little sherry just before serving.

Sweet potato chips

sweet potatoes, peeled and cut
  into chips
oil for deep-frying

Place sweet potatoes in a saucepan with salted water and bring to the boil. Reduce temperature and simmer for 1½ minutes. Drain sweet potatoes and pat dry. Heat oil until very hot, and deep-fry sweet potatoes. Drain chips on paper towel, then sprinkle with salt (or cinnamon sugar for variation). Serve immediately.

Sweet potatoes with marshmallows
Serves 4–6

5 sweet potatoes
4 tablespoons margarine
½ cup milk
1 teaspoon salt
1 tablespoon sugar
6 marshmallows, halved

Peel sweet potatoes and simmer in salted water until soft. Mash. Mix all remaining ingredients, except marshmallows, with the sweet potatoes. Spoon into a heavy-based saucepan, arrange marshmallows on top, cover saucepan and place on a grid over medium-hot coals for about 10 minutes, or until dish is warm and marshmallows melted.

Carrots and potatoes

Peel and boil equal quantities of carrots and potatoes in lightly salted water. As soon as vegetables are soft, drain water and mash vegetables with a little margarine. Add either a little black pepper or a little sugar, mix and serve hot.

Stewed green beans
Serves 4

3 cups green beans, sliced
1 potato, peeled and chopped
1 onion, chopped
salt to taste

Place the beans, potato and onion in a saucepan with a little salted water. Bring to the boil and simmer until the potato is soft. The vegetables can either be mashed or served as is. A little melted margarine or a dash of olive oil adds to the flavour.

Cauliflower curry
Serves 6

1 onion, finely chopped
3 tablespoons margarine
1 tablespoon masala or
  curry powder
1 teaspoon ground mustard
  seeds
½ teaspoon ground chilli
½ teaspoon ground turmeric
1 small cauliflower, broken
  into florets
salt to taste
½ cup water

Soften onion in margarine. Add spices and cauliflower and stir-fry for 4 minutes. Add salt and water. Cook, uncovered, until water has evaporated and cauliflower is tender.

Cauliflower au gratin
Serves 6–8

1 cauliflower, broken into
  florets
1 cup white sauce (see page 93)
½ cup grated Cheddar cheese
pinch of mustard powder
salt and pepper to taste

Cook cauliflower in salted water
for 15 minutes until tender.
Drain. Prepare white sauce and
stir in the cheese and mustard.
Season to taste. Mix sauce lightly
with the cauliflower.

Cauliflower with chilli-garlic dressing
Serves 6–8

1 small cauliflower, chopped
½ cup sunflower seeds
1 teaspoon dried chives

CHILLI-GARLIC DRESSING
½ cup oil
3 teaspoons chilli sauce
2 tablespoons red wine vinegar
3 cloves garlic, crushed

Boil cauliflower until just tender.
Drain and mix with sunflower
seeds and chives.
  Combine ingredients for
dressing in a screw-top jar and
shake well. Add dressing to
cauliflower and mix lightly.
Can be served warm or cold.

Sweetcorn fritters
Serves 4–6

1 x 410 g can creamed
  sweetcorn
1 egg, beaten
1 teaspoon salt
pinch of pepper
1 cup self-raising flour
oil for frying

Mix sweetcorn, egg, seasoning and
flour. Fry tablespoon measures of
the mixture in hot oil until brown
on both sides. Also delicious for
breakfast, served with syrup.

Corn fritters
Serves 4

2 eggs, separated
1 x 410 g can corn kernels,
  drained
dash of Worcestershire sauce
salt and pepper to taste
¾ cup plain (cake) flour
½ teaspoon baking powder
oil for frying

Beat egg whites until stiff and set
aside. In another bowl, combine
egg yolks, corn, Worcestershire
sauce and seasoning and mix well.
Stir in flour and baking powder.
Fold in egg whites. Heat oil in a
frying pan and drop in spoonfuls
of corn mixture. Turn and brown
on both sides. Drain well on paper
towel before serving.

Corn potjie
Serves 6

1¼ cups milk
2 tablespoons margarine
3 eggs, separated
1 x 410 g can corn kernels
1 cup grated Cheddar cheese
1 teaspoon French mustard
1 cup white breadcrumbs
salt and black pepper to taste

Heat milk and margarine. Beat egg yolks and add to milk with remaining ingredients, except the egg whites. Beat egg whites until stiff and fold in lightly. Cover saucepan and simmer slowly for 30 minutes over low heat until set.

HANDY HINT
Add a pinch of salt to powdered milk to improve the taste. To make 1 cup of milk, mix 4 tablespoons milk powder with 1 cup water.

Cabbage stir-fry
Serves 4

½ cabbage
3 carrots
1 onion
2 tablespoons oil
2 tablespoons seedless raisins
½ teaspoon dried marjoram
pinch of brown sugar
salt and pepper to taste
¼ cup chopped nuts
½ cup natural yoghurt

Shred the cabbage. Finely slice the carrots and onion. Heat oil in a large frying pan and stir-fry vegetables and raisins for about 5 minutes. Mix marjoram, sugar, seasoning and nuts into yoghurt and stir into vegetables. Heat gently, then serve immediately.

Asparagus with egg sauce
Serves 4

1 x 439 g can whole asparagus
  spears

SAUCE
1 egg, separated
½ teaspoon mustard powder
1 tablespoon sugar
¼ teaspoon salt
2 tablespoons vinegar
2 tablespoons liquid from
  asparagus

Heat asparagus in its own liquid, then drain and reserve liquid. Keep asparagus warm.

To prepare the sauce, whip all the sauce ingredients together. Place in a bowl over boiling water and stir until sauce thickens. Allow to cool slightly, then spoon over asparagus.

Ratatouille
Serves 6–8

2 onions, chopped
2 green peppers, seeded and
  chopped
1 clove garlic, crushed
2 tablespoons oil
1 carrot, diced
4 tomatoes, chopped
3 cups sliced baby marrows
  (courgettes)
2 teaspoons salt
½ teaspoon dried origanum
¼ teaspoon pepper

Fry onions, green peppers and garlic in oil until soft. Add remaining ingredients and simmer for approximately 15 minutes, or until vegetables are just tender (add a little water if necessary). Serve warm with rice.

Salads and Dressings

Most people on safari travel with a portable refrigerator or freezer, and therefore a few salads have been included which have a gelatine base and must be left in a cool place to set. The same effect can also be obtained with a good-quality cooler box and ice. Obviously, these salads are unsuitable if you do not have cooling facilities.

Some vegetables and fruit travel better than others. Use those that don't during the first few days and keep the cabbages, apples, etc. for later. Wilted vegetables, such as carrots or lettuce, can be revived by soaking them in ice-cold water for an hour or more.

Improvise if you do not have all the ingredients required for a recipe. Salads form the bulk of meals on safari and it is therefore important to pack enough fresh vegetables and fruit as well as a variety of canned foods to be able to prepare interesting salads. Some of the salads for lunch can be prepared the previous night or in the morning before breaking camp. Where this is not possible, pack all the ingredients in the lunchbox and prepare the salad fresh at the lunch spot.

Coleslaw with apples and carrots
Serves 4–6

1 tablespoon sunflower seeds
2 tablespoons orange juice
1 tablespoon oil
1 tablespoon vinegar
1 teaspoon honey
½ teaspoon dried basil
1 cup washed and finely
  shredded cabbage
2 apples, grated
1 cup peeled and grated carrots

Soak the sunflower seeds in orange juice for 1 hour (or put them together in a screw-top container in the morning so it can be ready for lunch). Mix together the oil, vinegar, honey and basil, then add the cabbage, apples and carrots and toss thoroughly so that they become well coated. Sprinkle the sunflower seeds over the salad.

Coleslaw with mixed vegetables
Serves 6–8

¼ cabbage, finely shredded
1 x 439 g can mixed vegetables,
  drained
¾ cup diced pineapple
3 bananas, sliced

DRESSING
½ cup condensed milk
2 tablespoons white vinegar
1 tablespoon oil
1 teaspoon mustard powder
1 egg yolk
½ teaspoon salt

Toss salad ingredients together
in a serving bowl.
  Mix ingredients for dressing
together and stir for about
2 minutes. Spoon over salad
and mix through.

Cool coleslaw
Serves 8–10

1 small cabbage, grated or
  shredded
2 stalks celery, chopped
  (optional)
1 cucumber, diced
1 cup sunflower seeds
½ cup sesame seeds
1 cup mayonnaise

Mix all ingredients together
and serve.

Coleslaw with fruit
Serves 8–10

1 small cabbage, grated or
  shredded
1 pineapple, peeled and grated
4 red apples, cored and diced
  (do not peel)
1 small packet seedless raisins
1 cup mayonnaise (or more,
  depending on size of cabbage)

Mix all ingredients together
and serve.

Coleslaw
Serves 6–8

¼ red cabbage, shredded
¼ green cabbage, shredded
1 small packet vacuum-packed
  croutons

DRESSING
½ cup natural yoghurt
4 tablespoons mayonnaise
dash of dry white wine
dash of lemon juice
salt and black pepper to taste

Mix cabbage and croutons in
a salad bowl.
  Thoroughly mix all the
ingredients for the dressing
and toss with the salad.

Coleslaw with curried beans
Serves 8–10

1 small cabbage, grated or
  shredded
2 cups curried beans
  (see page 102)

Simply mix together and serve.

Coleslaw with orange and granadilla
Serves 8–10

1 tablespoon honey
1 cup orange juice
1 small cabbage, grated or
  shredded
1 cup salted peanuts
1 cup seedless raisins
1 x 115 g can granadilla pulp

Dissolve honey in orange juice
and pour over cabbage. Mix in
peanuts and raisins. Put salad into
a serving bowl and garnish with
granadilla pulp.

Cabbage and asparagus salad
Serves 6–8

¼ cabbage
1 x 439 g can asparagus spears,
  drained
½ cup grated cheese
¼ cup mayonnaise or
  French dressing

Slice the cabbage thinly. Add
asparagus, cheese and mayonnaise
or French dressing. Stir to combine.

Rice salad with peaches 1
Serves 10

3 cups rice, cooked
1 x 410 g can peach slices,
  drained (if not available,
  substitute with other fruit,
  for example apricots)
1 green pepper, seeded and
  chopped
1 small onion, chopped
½ x 440 g can crushed
  pineapple
¼ cup sultanas
¼ cup seedless raisins

DRESSING
½ cup condensed milk
½ cup mayonnaise
¼ cup yoghurt (preferably
  peach or apricot flavour)
¼ cup chutney
2 tablespoons vinegar
1 teaspoon mustard powder
2 teaspoons curry powder
2 teaspoons turmeric
salt and pepper to taste

Mix all salad ingredients together.
  Mix all ingredients for dressing
and pour over salad.
  Should you want to prepare the
salad the previous night (for lunch
the next day), keep the dressing in
a separate container and mix it
into the salad just before serving,
as it tends to dry out if prepared
too long in advance.

Rice salad with peaches 2
Serves 6–8

1 cup rice, uncooked
1 onion, chopped
½ cup mayonnaise
2 teaspoons chutney
1 x 410 g can peach slices,
  drained
1 green pepper, seeded and
  chopped
¼ cup vinegar
¾ teaspoon curry powder

Boil rice in lightly salted water
until soft. Drain and add all the
other ingredients. This salad can
be made well in advance if kept
in a cooler box.

HANDY HINT
Try to improvise if ingredients
are not available. For example,
using peaches in a salad instead
of apricots will not affect the taste
and may mean the difference
between not preparing the dish
at all or improvising and preparing
a delicious salad.

Rice salad with fruit
Serves 6–8

2 teaspoons curry powder
2 tablespoons margarine
2 cups rice, uncooked
salt to taste
water
½ cup sliced banana
½ cup grated pineapple
1 cup mayonnaise
nuts, chopped

Fry curry powder in margarine for 2 minutes. Add rice and stir-fry for 3 minutes. Add salt and enough water to cover rice and leave to boil until rice is tender. Remove from heat and leave to cool completely. Layer rice with banana and pineapple in a bowl and pour mayonnaise over (or Sweet dressing 1, see page 87). Lift layers gently, without mixing the ingredients, to allow the dressing to trickle in between the layers. Top with nuts.

Spanish rice salad
Serves 8–10

2 cups rice, uncooked
½ cup vinegar
¾ cup oil
2 teaspoons curry powder
1 teaspoon mustard powder
2 cups tomato sauce
salt and pepper to taste
1 green pepper, seeded and
   chopped
1 onion, chopped

Cook rice in lightly salted water until soft. Drain and allow to cool. Whip vinegar, oil, curry powder, mustard and tomato sauce until well mixed. Stir into rice and add seasoning, green pepper and onion. The taste of this salad will improve if it is prepared well in advance and left in a refrigerator or cooler box for at least 1–2 hours.

Rice and lentil salad
Serves 4

½ cup rice, uncooked
½ cup lentils (brown or orange)
4 tomatoes, chopped
1 small onion, chopped
½ cup natural yoghurt
juice of ½ lemon
salt and pepper to taste

Cook rice and lentils separately in salted, boiling water. Drain, mix together and allow to cool. Stir in tomatoes, onion, yoghurt, lemon juice and seasoning.

Mango salad
Serves 4

1 x 410 g can mangoes
½ teaspoon flavoured seasoning (Maggi, Aromat)
¼ cup French dressing

Drain mangoes and reserve syrup. Sprinkle flavoured seasoning over mangoes. Mix ¼ cup reserved syrup with French dressing and pour over mangoes.

Curried mango salad
Serves 4

1 x 410 g can mangoes, drained

CURRY SAUCE
2 tablespoons curry powder
¼ teaspoon dried chilli
1 teaspoon salt
1 teaspoon turmeric
2 tablespoons sugar
¼ cup vinegar
2 bay leaves

Mix all the ingredients for the curry sauce together in a saucepan.
   Add mangoes and simmer gently over low heat for about 5 minutes. Allow to cool and remove bay leaves before serving.

Apple salad
Serves 4

1 lettuce (or ¼ cabbage),
  shredded
½ cup grated, bottled beetroot
  (without liquid)
2 apples, cored and diced
  (do not peel)
French dressing
1 stalk celery, sliced (optional)
1 onion, thinly sliced
nuts, chopped

Put lettuce (or cabbage), beetroot
and apples in a bowl and toss with
dressing. Add celery and onion
rings. Garnish with chopped nuts.

Easy pea salad
Serves 4–6

1 x 410 g can peas, drained
1 small pineapple, diced
mayonnaise

Mix the peas and pineapple
together and stir in enough
mayonnaise to lightly coat the
ingredients (about 1 tablespoon).

Stewed fruit salad 1
Serves 8–10

1 x 500 g packet mixed dried
  fruit
sweetened Rooibos tea
3 bananas, sliced

DRESSING
¾ cup stewed fruit yoghurt
3 tablespoons mayonnaise
4 tablespoons condensed milk

Soak dried fruit overnight in tea.
Bring to the boil, then reduce heat
and simmer in tea until fruit
softens. Remove from heat and
allow to cool. Drain. Add bananas.
  Mix all dressing ingredients
together and stir into fruit
mixture. Serve immediately.

Stewed fruit salad 2
Serves 8–10

1 x 500 g packet mixed dried
  fruit
water
1 x 397 g can condensed milk
¼ cup vinegar
¼ cup oil
1 teaspoon mustard powder

Place fruit in a saucepan with just
enough water to cover, then bring
to the boil. Reduce heat and simmer until the fruit softens (about
30 minutes). Leave to cool. Drain.
Mix the remaining ingredients
together and pour over the fruit.

Beetroot salad
Serves 4–6

2 cups diced beetroot
½ cup peas
½ cup diced pineapple
1 tablespoon grated onion

DRESSING
¼ cup sugar
1¼ tablespoons cornflour
⅓ cup vinegar
¼ cup water
2 tablespoons margarine
½ teaspoon salt

Mix all the salad ingredients
together and set aside.
  To make the dressing, mix all
ingredients together and simmer
gently for about 5 minutes over
low heat. Allow to cool before
pouring over salad.

Beetroot with fruit
Serves 8–10

780 g (1 bottle) grated, bottled
  beetroot
2 apples (or 2 bananas)

Simply open a bottle of grated
beetroot and empty it into an
attractive bowl. Add either grated
apples or sliced bananas and serve.

Beetroot mould
Serves 6–8

2 cups water
salt and pepper to taste
3 tablespoons vinegar
1½ packets lemon jelly
1½ cups grated beetroot
3 tablespoons grated onion

Bring water, seasoning and vinegar
to the boil. Remove from heat
and add jelly. Stir until jelly has
dissolved, then leave to cool.
Stir in beetroot and onion, then
pour into a mould that has been
rinsed with cold water. Place in
a refrigerator or cold cooler box
until salad has set. Turn out onto
a plate before serving.
  If desired, the salad can be
served with whipped cream that
has been sweetened with a little
sugar. This salad is delicious and
looks very impressive, especially
if you spend Christmas day in
the bush!

Macaroni salad 1
Serves 8

1 x 500 g packet macaroni
1 tomato, chopped
½ cup grated Cheddar cheese

DRESSING
1 egg yolk
1 tablespoon white vinegar
1 tablespoon honey
1 teaspoon mustard powder
1 teaspoon salt
½ cup water
3 tablespoons oil

Cook macaroni in lightly
salted water until soft and allow
to cool completely. Add tomato
and cheese.
   To prepare the dressing, whip
the egg yolk, vinegar, honey,
mustard, salt and water together.
Place in a bowl over boiling water
and stir until sauce coats the
spoon. Remove from heat and stir
in oil very gradually until all the
oil is used and the sauce thickens.
Allow to cool before mixing it
into the macaroni.

Macaroni salad 2
Serves 8

1 x 500 g packet macaroni,
   cooked in salted water
1 cup chopped celery (optional)
¾ cup grated cabbage
2 teaspoons dried parsley
1 tablespoon lemon juice
½ teaspoon salt
¼ teaspoon paprika
1 cup mayonnaise

Mix all ingredients together
and serve.

Cucumber bites
Serves 4–6

1 English cucumber, diced
1 tablespoon finely chopped
   dates
1 tablespoon grated onion
pinch of garlic salt
1 tablespoon lemon juice
1 teaspoon brown sugar
1 x 175 ml tub natural yoghurt

Mix all ingredients together
and serve.

Cucumber mould 1
Serves 6–8

2 tablespoons gelatine
¼ cup cold water
1 x 410 g can crushed pineapple
1 tablespoon sugar
1 cucumber, peeled and
  grated (preferably not
  English variety)
1 cup grated Cheddar cheese
½ cup mayonnaise
1 onion, grated
salt and pepper to taste

Soak gelatine in half of the water. Bring remaining water, pineapple and sugar to the boil. Add gelatine and stir until dissolved. Allow to cool. Add remaining ingredients and mix well. Pour into a mould that has been rinsed with cold water and leave in refrigerator or cold cooler box until set.

Cucumber mould 2
Serves 6–8

1 x 80 g packet greengage jelly
1 cup boiling water
1 cup mayonnaise
1 x 250 g tub smooth
  cottage cheese
2 cucumbers, peeled and
  grated (preferably not
  English variety)
1 small onion, grated
2 teaspoons lemon juice
salt and pepper to taste

Dissolve jelly in boiling water and allow to cool. Add remaining ingredients and mix. Pour into a mould that has been rinsed with cold water and place in refrigerator or cold cooler box until set.

Cucumber with yoghurt

Peel and finely slice the required amount of cucumber. Leave to stand for a while and pour off any liquid that has accumulated. Sprinkle with salt and coarse black pepper and cover with natural yoghurt. Serve chilled with a curry dish.

Potato salad
Serves 6

6 large potatoes, cooked with
 skins
4 rashers bacon, cut into small
 pieces
1 onion, grated
1 clove garlic, crushed
1 apple, diced (do not peel)
1 tablespoon lemon juice

DRESSING
1 cup mayonnaise
1 egg yolk
2 tablespoons vinegar
1 tablespoon French mustard
1 teaspoon salt
¼ teaspoon pepper
1 teaspoon brown sugar

Peel potatoes and cut into slices.
Arrange in an attractive bowl.
Fry bacon until crisp and spoon
over potatoes (including the
bacon dripping). Add the onion,
garlic, apple and lemon juice.
 Prepare dressing by mixing all
the ingredients together and pour
over the potatoes, mixing lightly.
The taste of this salad improves
if it is eaten the next day.

Potato salad with sweet dressing
Serves 4

6 medium potatoes, cooked and
 thinly sliced

DRESSING
½ teaspoon mustard powder
½ teaspoon salt
¼ teaspoon pepper
½ cup condensed milk
1 egg yolk
¼ cup oil
¼ cup vinegar

Mix the dry dressing ingredients
and add to the condensed milk.
Whip the egg yolk and stir it
into the condensed milk; then
the oil, and lastly the vinegar.
Leave to stand for a few minutes
in a cool place to thicken.
 Alternate potatoes and dressing
in layers in a bowl.

Crunchy bacon salad
Serves 4

3 tablespoons margarine
5 tablespoons oil
4 thick slices white bread, cubed
8 rashers rindless bacon, cut into small pieces
1 cup sliced mushrooms
½ small onion, grated
salt and pepper to taste
pinch of mustard powder
1 tablespoon vinegar
¼ cup pimento-stuffed green olives, sliced

Heat the margarine and 2 tablespoons of the oil and fry the bread cubes until crisp and golden. Drain on absorbent paper towel. Fry the bacon in the same pan until crisp. Drain well. Add mushrooms to the pan and cook until soft. Drain and place in a salad bowl. Add onion, seasoning and mustard. Blend the remaining oil and vinegar into the mushroom mixture and leave to cool. Stir in the olives, bacon and croutons and serve immediately.

Ham and egg salad
Serves 4

1 lettuce, washed and broken into small pieces
2 cups diced cooked ham
1 x 312 g can mandarin oranges, drained
2 tablespoons mayonnaise
3 hard-boiled eggs, sliced
1 green pepper, seeded and cut into rings

Arrange the lettuce in a bowl. Mix ham with the mandarin oranges and some of the mayonnaise. Spoon mixture into a bowl and top with remaining mayonnaise, eggs and green pepper.

Broccoli and egg salad
Serves 4

450 g broccoli
2 tomatoes, quartered
6 spring onions (or 1 onion),
  chopped
4 tablespoons mayonnaise
2 hard-boiled eggs, sliced
salt to taste
paprika

Break the broccoli into sprigs
and cook in lightly salted water
until tender. Drain and place in
a serving bowl. Add tomatoes,
spring onions and mayonnaise
and mix. Garnish salad with
sliced eggs and sprinkle with salt
and paprika.

Nutty cheese salad
Serves 4–6

4 apples, sliced
juice of 1 lemon
¼ cup chopped walnuts
  (or any other nuts)
¼ cup sultanas
¼ cup chopped celery
  (optional)
¼ cabbage, shredded
1 cup grated Cheddar cheese
salt and pepper to taste
½ cup natural yoghurt

Sprinkle apples with lemon juice.
Mix in the walnuts, sultanas, celery,
cabbage, cheese, salt and pepper.
Add yoghurt and mix lightly.

Pear salad
Serves 4

1 x 825 g can pear halves
3 tablespoons cream cheese
1 tablespoon lemon juice
2 tablespoons chopped nuts
mayonnaise

Drain pears and reserve syrup.
Mash half of the pears until
smooth. Blend cream cheese
with lemon juice and enough of
the pear syrup to form a creamy
consistency. Mix with the mashed
pears. Fill the cavities of the
remaining pear halves with the
mixture and sprinkle with nuts.
Serve with mayonnaise.

Easy peach salad
Serves 6

1 x 410 g can peach slices,
  drained
¼ x 390 g bottle piccalilli
  (pickled mixed vegetables)

Mix peaches and piccalilli together
and serve, preferably well-chilled.

Salad Niçoise
Serves 6

1 x 210 g can tuna, drained
  and flaked
1 green pepper, seeded and
  sliced
1 tablespoon chopped onion
3 tomatoes, cut into wedges
1 cup French beans, cooked
  (or substitute with canned
  green beans)
6 tablespoons French dressing
3 hard-boiled eggs, quartered
½ can anchovy fillets, drained
black olives

Lightly toss the tuna, green
pepper, onion, tomatoes, beans
and dressing. Arrange the eggs,
anchovy fillets and black olives
on top of the salad and serve.

Cheese and orange salad
Serves 4

1 lettuce (or ½ small cabbage,
  grated)
2 oranges, peeled and
  segmented
1 cup diced Cheddar cheese
2 tablespoons cashew nuts
1 tablespoon olive oil
1 tablespoon lemon juice
salt and pepper to taste

Wash and dry lettuce, then tear
it coarsely and arrange in a salad
bowl. Add oranges, cheese and
nuts. Dress with olive oil and
lemon juice and add seasoning.

Three-bean salad
Serves 8–10

2 onions, chopped
2 rashers bacon, chopped
1 green pepper, seeded and
  chopped
2 cloves garlic, crushed
1 teaspoon ground ginger
2 teaspoons curry powder
1 tablespoon oil
3 tomatoes, chopped
salt and pepper to taste
½ teaspoon sugar
1 bay leaf
1 x 410 g can baked beans
  in tomato sauce
1 x 410 g can butter beans (or
  red kidney beans), drained
1 x 410 g can green beans,
  drained

Fry onions, bacon, green pepper,
garlic, ginger and curry powder
in oil. Add tomatoes, seasoning,
sugar and bay leaf and simmer
for about 10 minutes. Remove
from heat and discard bay leaf.
Add all the beans and mix well
with the sauce. The salad can
be served warm or cold. The
flavour improves if prepared
a day in advance.

Butter bean salad
Serves 6

½ cup sliced salami
2 x 410 g cans butter beans,
  drained
1 tomato, chopped
1 onion, chopped
1 teaspoon dried basil
1 hard-boiled egg, chopped
1 anchovy fillet, chopped

DRESSING
¼ cup olive oil
2 tablespoons vinegar
½ teaspoon sugar

Cut salami into thin strips and
combine with beans, tomato,
onion and basil in a bowl. Mix
well. Top with egg and anchovy.
  Combine ingredients for dressing
in a screw-top jar, shake well and
pour over salad.

Bean and sweetcorn salad
Serves 6

1 x 410 g can kidney beans,
  drained
1 x 410 g can sweetcorn
  kernels, drained
2 onions, chopped

DRESSING
2 tablespoons white vinegar
4 tablespoons oil
½ teaspoon salt
¼ teaspoon pepper
1 teaspoon dried rosemary

Mix beans, sweetcorn and onion together in a bowl.

Combine all the dressing ingredients in a screw-top jar and shake well. Stir the dressing into the salad.

Red bean salad
Serves 6

1 x 410 g can red beans,
  drained
1 x 410 g can corn kernels,
  drained
1 green pepper, seeded and
  chopped

DRESSING
½ cup vinegar
½ teaspoon ground cumin
1 fresh green chilli (or
  substitute with ½ teaspoon
  dried chilli)
½ cup oil

Mix all salad ingredients in a bowl.

To prepare the dressing, put all ingredients in a screw-top jar and shake together for about 2 minutes before pouring over the salad.

Tuna bean salad
Serves 4–6

1 tablespoon lemon juice
2 apples, chopped (do not peel)
1 x 210 g can tuna, drained
   and flaked
1 tablespoon chopped onion
3 stalks celery, sliced (optional)
1 x 410 g can red kidney beans,
   drained
salt and pepper to taste
4 tablespoons French dressing

Sprinkle lemon juice over the
apples, then add tuna, onion,
celery and beans. Season well, add
the dressing and toss thoroughly.
Leave to stand for about
30 minutes before serving.

Bean salad
Serves 4–6

2 onions, chopped
2 tablespoons margarine
2 tablespoons oil
1 x 410 g can baked beans in
   tomato sauce
2 eggs, beaten
2 tablespoons vinegar
pinch of salt
2 teaspoons sugar

Fry onions in margarine and oil
until soft. Add rest of ingredients
and simmer for 3 minutes,
stirring continuously. Allow
to cool before serving.

Bean salad with vegetables
Serves 6

1 x 410 g can baked beans in
   tomato sauce
1 cup grated carrots
¾ cup grated cabbage
1 tomato, chopped
¼ onion, chopped
salt and pepper to taste
½ cup mayonnaise, mixed
   with ¼ cup milk

Mix all ingredients together
and serve.

Bean salad with pineapple
Serves 6

1 x 410 g can baked beans in
   tomato sauce
½ pineapple, diced
2 teaspoons Worcestershire
   sauce
2 tablespoons vinegar
1 tablespoon sugar
¼ teaspoon celery salt

Mix all ingredients together
in a salad bowl and place in a
cooler box or refrigerator for
1 hour. Serve.

Banana salad
Serves 4

lemon juice
3 bananas, peeled and cut
  lengthways
apricot jam
mayonnaise, mixed with
  a little milk
chopped walnuts

Sprinkle lemon juice over the bananas and smear each half with apricot jam. Arrange in a flat dish and spoon mayonnaise over. Sprinkle with nuts.

HANDY HINT
To prevent bananas from turning black in a salad or dessert, submerge them in freshly boiled water for about 3 minutes. The skins will turn black, but the bananas will remain perfect inside. This method also produces better results than sprinkling the fruit with lemon juice.

Banana mould
Serves 6–8

1 x 80 g packet lemon jelly
1 cup boiling water
1 x 397 g can condensed milk
½ cup white vinegar
¼ teaspoon mustard powder
salt and pepper to taste
1 x 410 g can peas, drained
3 bananas, sliced

Dissolve jelly in boiling water and leave to cool completely. Mix condensed milk, vinegar, mustard and seasoning. Stir in peas, bananas and jelly, then pour into a mould that has been rinsed with cold water. Place in the refrigerator or cold cooler box until salad has set. Turn out onto a plate before serving.

Chicken salad
Serves 6

1 chicken, cooked, deboned and
 chopped into small pieces
1 cucumber, diced
1 cup natural yoghurt
1 teaspoon lemon juice
2 tablespoons chopped onion
salt and pepper to taste

Mix all ingredients together
and serve.

Chicken cream
Serves 6

2 cups cooked and diced
 chicken
1 cup grated pineapple
¼ cup pecan nuts, chopped
1 cup cream, whipped
1 cup mayonnaise

Mix chicken, pineapple and
nuts, then fold in the cream and
mayonnaise. Chill well before
serving.

Chicken salad with pears
Serves 4

2 cups cooked, deboned and
 diced chicken
1 x 410 g can pears, drained
 and diced
½ cup chopped pecan nuts

DRESSING
½ cup thick cream
1 tablespoon sugar
¼ teaspoon salt
pinch of pepper
1 tablespoon vinegar

Mix all salad ingredients together.
 To prepare the dressing, whip
cream until it begins to thicken.
Add sugar, salt and pepper and
mix thoroughly. Add vinegar and
whip for about 3 minutes. Pour
over salad ingredients and gently
mix in.

Chicken salad with apricots
Serves 4–6

¼ cup natural yoghurt
5 canned apricots, sliced
4 chicken breasts, skinned,
  cooked and diced
2 stalks celery, sliced (optional)
1 teaspoon dried chives
salt and black pepper to taste
2 tablespoons flaked almonds

MAYONNAISE (MAKES 1 CUP)
1 egg
2 tablespoons lemon juice
1 teaspoon mustard powder
pinch of salt
black pepper to taste
1 cup oil
1 tablespoon warm water
  (if necessary)

To make the mayonnaise, place egg, lemon juice, mustard and seasoning in a bowl and whisk for 1 minute. Add oil drop by drop (otherwise mayonnaise will curdle), stirring all the time. If mixture is too thick, thin down with the warm water.

Combine the mayonnaise with yoghurt. Add apricots, chicken, celery, chives and seasoning, toss lightly and chill. Scatter almonds over the top.

Chicken salad with peaches
Serves 6

1 onion, chopped
1 green pepper, seeded and
  chopped
1 tablespoon oil
1 teaspoon curry powder
3 cups cooked, deboned and
  diced chicken
1 cup mayonnaise
salt and pepper to taste
1 x 410 g can peach slices,
  drained

Fry onion and green pepper in oil until soft. Add curry powder and fry for another 2 minutes. Leave to cool and add to the remaining ingredients.

Russian salad
Serves 4

½ cup cooked and diced potato
1 cup cooked and diced
  cold meat
¼ cup cooked and diced
  beetroot
¼ cup diced cucumber
1 red apple, diced (do not peel)
½ teaspoon dried parsley
1 teaspoon finely chopped
  onion
salt and pepper to taste
mayonnaise
1 hard-boiled egg, sliced

Mix all the ingredients together,
except the egg. Serve with sliced
egg on top of salad as decoration.

Butternut salad
Serves 8–10

1 butternut, peeled and
  finely grated
1 x 410 g can apricots or
  peaches, drained and chopped
1 apple, peeled and diced
1 cup fruit juice (apricot or
  peach)

DRESSING
1 cup fruit yoghurt (apricot
  or peach)
¼ cup mayonnaise
¼ cup grated pineapple
¼ cup cream

Mix salad ingredients and chill.
  Combine all dressing ingredients
and pour over salad, gently lifting
salad with two spoons so dressing
can trickle through slightly.

Butternut with granadilla
Serves 6–8

1 teaspoon honey
¼ cup orange juice
1 butternut, peeled and
   coarsely grated
½ cup granadilla pulp
½ cup seedless raisins
¼ cup pecan nuts, chopped

Dissolve the honey in the
orange juice. Lightly mix all the
ingredients with the honey-juice
mixture and serve. Garnish with
more chopped nuts.

Marshmallow salad
Serves 6–8

¼ cup pecan nuts
1 cup diced pineapple
1 cup diced apple
1 cup marshmallows, cut into
   small pieces
½ cup chopped celery
   (optional)
½ cup chopped dates
3 cups shredded cabbage
vinaigrette dressing
   (see page 86)

Mix all ingredients together
and serve.

Sweet-and-sour carrots
Serves 8–10

1 kg carrots, sliced (or frozen
   baby carrots)
1 green pepper, seeded and
   sliced
2 onions, sliced

DRESSING
1 cup tomato purée
¾ cup vinegar
3 tablespoons oil
2 teaspoons Worcestershire
   sauce
1 cup sugar
½ teaspoon mustard powder
1 teaspoon salt
black pepper

Cook carrots until soft and arrange
in alternate layers in a salad bowl
with green pepper and onions.
   Mix all the dressing ingredients
in a saucepan and simmer for
about 5 minutes. Pour the dressing
over the salad while still hot. Leave
to cool, then place in a refrigerator
or cooler box. This salad should
be prepared well in advance (up
to 3 days is best) as the taste
improves with time.

Bread salad

Serves 6

1 loaf stale white bread, thickly
  sliced and crusts removed
oil for frying
1 cup diced cheese
1 x 440 g can pineapple pieces,
  drained
a few grapes, seeded
1 green pepper, seeded and
  chopped

SAUCE
1 x 397 g can condensed milk
¼ teaspoon mustard powder
2 tablespoons lemon juice
¼ cup mayonnaise

Cut the bread slices into cubes.
Deep-fry cubes in oil and drain
on absorbent paper towel. Mix
with remaining salad ingredients.
  Mix all ingredients for sauce
and pour over salad. Do not mix
the ingredients together too long
before serving, as the bread will
become soggy.

Avocado salad

Mix equal quantities of diced
avocado, tomato and bananas with
a small quantity of finely grated
onion. Season and serve with the
following dressing:

DRESSING
½ teaspoon mustard powder
½ teaspoon salt
¼ teaspoon pepper
½ cup condensed milk
1 egg yolk, beaten
¼ cup oil
¼ cup vinegar

Mix dry ingredients and add to
condensed milk. Add egg yolk,
then oil and lastly the vinegar.
Allow to stand in a cool place for
a while until thickened, then stir
into salad ingredients.

Sousboontjies
Serves 2–4

1 cup sugar beans
1 tablespoon vinegar
2 tablespoons margarine
2 tablespoons sugar
1 teaspoon salt
½ teaspoon pepper

Wash the beans and soak overnight. Drain and parboil in fresh water until almost soft, then add the remaining ingredients. Simmer, stirring continuously, until beans are cooked. Leave to cool, then serve.

Pasta salad
Serves 6–8

2 cups noodles, cooked
1 cup chopped salami
1 tomato, chopped
½ green pepper, seeded and chopped
½ onion, chopped

DRESSING
¾ cup mayonnaise
½ cup chutney
1 clove garlic, crushed
4 tablespoons cream (optional)

Mix the ingredients together for the salad.

In a separate bowl, combine the ingredients for the dressing. Pour over the pasta salad.

Salad Dressings

Basic vinaigrette dressing

1 part white wine vinegar
  (or fresh lemon juice)
salt
black pepper
mustard powder
crushed garlic
3 parts olive oil

Whisk the vinegar with salt, pepper, mustard and garlic. Gradually add the oil in a steady stream so the dressing emulsifies and thickens slightly. Taste for seasoning and adjust if necessary.

French dressing

1 tablespoon vinegar or
  lemon juice
¼ cup oil
pinch each of salt and pepper
¼ teaspoon mustard powder

Combine ingredients in a screw-top jar and shake well for a few minutes.

Honey and lemon dressing

¾ cup oil
¼ cup lemon juice
¼ cup clear honey
1 teaspoon grated onion
¼ teaspoon mustard powder
1 teaspoon paprika
1 teaspoon celery salt

Combine all the ingredients in a bowl and whisk. Leave to stand for 15 minutes, then whisk again before serving.

Sweet dressing 1

1 teaspoon mustard powder
½ teaspoon salt
¼ teaspoon pepper
½ cup condensed milk
1 egg yolk, beaten
¼ cup oil
¼ cup vinegar

Mix dry ingredients together and add condensed milk. Stir egg yolk into condensed milk mixture. Add oil and then the vinegar. Mix thoroughly and allow to stand for a few minutes to thicken.

Sweet dressing 2

¾ cup condensed milk
½ cup vinegar
½ teaspoon salt
½ teaspoon mustard powder
½ teaspoon paprika
½ cup green olives, chopped

Mix the condensed milk, vinegar, salt, mustard and paprika. Add the olives and beat until smooth. Leave for a few minutes in a cool place until dressing thickens.

Mayonnaise

2 egg yolks
pinch each of salt, pepper and
   mustard powder
1¼ cups oil
1½ tablespoons white wine
   vinegar
1½ tablespoons warm water

Beat the egg yolks with the salt, pepper and mustard. Gradually beat in the oil, drop by drop (it is very important that the oil is added drop by drop otherwise the mayonnaise will curdle), until the mixture thickens. Stir in a little vinegar. Continue adding the oil until it is all absorbed, beating in a little more vinegar every time the mayonnaise becomes thick. Gently stir in any remaining vinegar with the water.

Sauces and Marinades

Barbecue sauce or marinade

½ cup tomato sauce
¼ cup Worcestershire sauce
1 tablespoon chutney
1 teaspoon mustard powder
½ cup vinegar
1 tablespoon oil
1 clove garlic, crushed
1 tablespoon sugar
½ cup cream

Mix all the ingredients together and simmer gently for about 5 minutes. Delicious as a sauce or marinade for any meat or chicken dish.

Braai sauce for lamb

3 tablespoons soy sauce
3 tablespoons honey
3 tablespoons dry white wine
  or vinegar
1 teaspoon Worcestershire sauce
1 teaspoon prepared hot
  English mustard
1 teaspoon tomato paste
1 teaspoon lemon juice

Mix all the ingredients together and baste lamb frequently with the sauce during the last 10 minutes of the cooking process. The meat can also be served with the left-over sauce.

Garlic dip

1½ cups tomato sauce
½ cup Worcestershire sauce
1 cup oil
4 cloves garlic, crushed
1 tablespoon dried parsley
2 onions, grated
1 cup vinegar
salt and pepper to taste

Mix all the ingredients together
and stir frequently. The sauce
can be used as a dip or as a sauce
over meat. If kept in a refrigerator
or cooler box it will keep for
weeks and the taste improves
after a few days.

Mushroom sauce 1

2 tablespoons margarine
1 tablespoon oil
2 cups chopped mushrooms
2 small onions, chopped
2 tablespoons plain (cake) flour
2 teaspoons dried parsley
2 tablespoons sherry
3 tablespoons sour cream
salt to taste

Heat margarine and oil and fry
mushrooms and onions for a
few minutes. Stir in flour and
allow to simmer for a further
2 minutes. Add parsley, sherry,
sour cream and salt. Serve
immediately. Delicious with
meat, chicken, baked potatoes,
pasta and pancakes.

Mushroom sauce 2

1 tablespoon finely chopped
  onion
1 tablespoon margarine
½ cup milk
1 x 425 g can mushroom soup

Brown onion in margarine. Blend
milk and soup, then stir into
onion mixture. Heat thoroughly
before serving. Delicious with
meat, chicken, baked potatoes,
pasta and pancakes.

Meat marinade

½ cup oil
1½ cups dry wine (red or white)
1 clove garlic, crushed
1 onion, chopped
pepper to taste

Mix all the ingredients together
and marinade meat in the sauce
for 6 hours or more. Can also be
used for chicken.

Sweet-and-sour sauce 1

½ cup tomato sauce
¼ cup honey
2 teaspoons Worcestershire
  sauce
1 tablespoon soy sauce
1 tablespoon white vinegar

Mix all the ingredients together
and baste chicken with sauce.

Sweet-and-sour sauce 2

1 cup pineapple juice
pinch of ground ginger
1 tablespoon soy sauce
2 tablespoons vinegar
1½ tablespoons brown sugar
2 tablespoons cornflour

Mix all the ingredients and
simmer for about 3 minutes to
cook cornflour. Delicious served
with stir-fried vegetables or
meat cubes.

Cool cucumber sauce

½ cucumber, grated
½ cup natural yoghurt
1 teaspoon dried dill
1 teaspoon lemon juice
pinch each of salt and pepper

Mix all the ingredients together
and place in a refrigerator or cooler
box to chill. Serve with curry or
any kind of meat.

Apple sauce

6 green apples, peeled and
  chopped
½ cup water
rind of ¼ lemon
½ cup sugar

Simmer apples gently in water
with lemon rind and sugar. When
apples are soft, mash them and
cook again until sauce thickens.
Discard lemon rind before serving.
Will compliment pork dishes.

Red wine sauce with mushrooms

½ cup chopped onion
1 cup chopped mushrooms
2 tablespoons margarine
1½ cups meat extract (or a
  bouillon cube)
½ cup dry red wine
2 teaspoons plain (cake) flour

Fry onion and mushrooms in
margarine. Add meat extract and
wine and simmer for 20 minutes.
Mix flour with a little cold water
and stir into the mushroom
mixture. Simmer for a further
4 minutes. Delicious with steaks.

Cold mustard sauce 1

¾ cup evaporated milk
3 teaspoons mustard powder
1 onion, finely chopped
2 teaspoons sugar
pinch of salt

Mix all the ingredients together
and serve cold with cold meats
or chicken.

Cold mustard sauce 2

¼ cup Old Cape prepared
  mustard
3 tablespoons brandy
½ cup natural yoghurt
½ cup mayonnaise
salt to taste

Mix all the ingredients together
and serve with cold meats.

Warm mustard sauce

Serves 2

2 tablespoons margarine
1 teaspoon mustard powder
1 teaspoon Worcestershire sauce
½ cup thick cream

Melt margarine and stir in mustard powder and Worcestershire sauce. Add cream and mix well. Serve warm with any meat dish.

Chilled garlic sauce

1 cup natural yoghurt
½ cup dry white wine
6 cloves garlic, crushed
salt and pepper to taste

Mix all the ingredients together and serve cold. Delicious with raw vegetables.

Chutney sauce

1 cup cream cheese
2 tablespoons chutney
1 tablespoon lemon juice
2 teaspoons tomato sauce
5 tablespoons cream

Mix all the ingredients together and serve cold.

Delicious sauce for braaipap

2 onions, chopped
2 cloves garlic, crushed
2 tablespoons margarine
5 tomatoes, chopped
1 apple, peeled and grated
½ cup sultanas
½ cup white wine
1 teaspoon sugar
1 teaspoon salt
pinch of pepper

Fry onion and garlic in margarine until light brown. Add remaining ingredients and simmer for about 10 minutes. Serve hot.

White sauce

2 tablespoons margarine
2 tablespoons plain (cake) flour
1 cup milk
salt and pepper to taste
pinch of grated nutmeg

Melt the margarine and add the flour whilst stirring constantly. Pour in the milk, about ¼ cup at a time, stirring all the time. When all the milk is added, bring to the boil, then simmer slowly for about 2 minutes. Season to taste and add nutmeg. For a thicker sauce, add another tablespoon each margarine and flour. Alternatively, if you prefer a thinner sauce, add more milk.

Cheese sauce

Stir ½ cup grated Cheddar cheese into white sauce (see above), then add ¼ teaspoon mustard powder or cayenne pepper.

Onion sauce

Stir a small, finely grated onion into white sauce (see above).

Béchamel sauce

2 tablespoons margarine
2 tablespoons plain (cake) flour
2 cups milk
1 bay leaf
1 blade mace
1 slice onion
salt and pepper

Melt margarine in a saucepan. Stir in flour and cook for 1 minute. Gradually add milk that has been infused with bay leaf, mace and onion. Strain and cook for 2 minutes. Season to taste.

Hot Tabasco® sauce

½ teaspoon mustard powder
1 cup tomato juice
1 tablespoon vinegar
2 tablespoons brown sugar
1 tablespoon oil
1 tablespoon lemon juice
salt and pepper to taste
1 small onion, chopped
1 teaspoon Tabasco® sauce

Mix the mustard with the tomato juice. Add remaining ingredients and mix well. Use as a basting sauce for steaks or lamb chops.

Vegetarian Dishes

Lentil dahl
Serves 4

2 onions, chopped
1 clove garlic, crushed
2 tablespoons oil
4 carrots, peeled and grated
1½ cups brown lentils
1 tablespoon curry powder
salt to taste
1 teaspoon brown sugar
2 tablespoons tomato purée
2 cups vegetable stock
lemon juice

Fry the onions and garlic in the oil until brown. Add the carrots and lentils and stir well, then add the curry powder and cook gently for a few minutes. Add salt, sugar, tomato purée and stock and stir until boiling. Reduce heat and simmer gently for about 45 minutes, or until lentils are cooked. Add a little lemon juice and adjust seasoning if necessary. Serve with rice.

Soya stew
Serves 8

1 onion, chopped
1 tablespoon oil
1 x 120 g packet soya mince, curry flavour
3 cups water
1 x 440 g can pineapple pieces
1 cup seedless raisins
8 potatoes, cooked and quartered
1 teaspoon ground coriander
2 tablespoons chutney

Fry onions in oil until brown. Add soya mince and water and simmer over very low heat for 10 minutes. Add remaining ingredients and simmer for another 10 minutes.

Savoury mince
Serves 6–8

6 cups water
1 x 120 g packet soya mince,
  savoury flavour
1 vegetable stock cube
2 teaspoons curry powder
2 teaspoons garlic flakes
1 x 27 g packet vegetable soup
2 tablespoons sugar
4 tablespoons raisins
1 bay leaf
¼ teaspoon grated nutmeg
¼ teaspoon ground ginger
¼ teaspoon ground cinnamon
1 cup rice, uncooked

Bring water to the boil and add
all ingredients, including the rice.
Simmer for 30–40 minutes, or
until rice is cooked.

Bean pie
Serves 4

1 x 410 g can baked beans in
  tomato sauce
1 tablespoon oats
½ cup grated Cheddar cheese
pinch of salt
1 egg, beaten
½ cup breadcrumbs
½ cup melted margarine

Mash the beans slightly with a
fork and add the oats, half the
cheese and the salt. Mix well
then add egg. Spoon mixture into
a greased, fireproof pot. Sprinkle
remaining cheese with breadcrumbs
and margarine over the top, cover
with lid and bake over medium-
hot coals (put a few on the lid as
well) for about 30 minutes.

Vegetarian bobotie with lentils
Serves 4–6

2 cups brown lentils
2 onions, chopped
1 tablespoon margarine
1 tablespoon oil
1¼ cups milk
3 large eggs
2 slices white bread (crusts removed), cubed
½ cup finely chopped dried apricots
1 large apple, peeled and grated
¼ cup sultanas or seedless raisins
¼ cup blanched almonds
3 tablespoons apricot jam
2 teaspoons curry powder
2 tablespoons lemon juice
salt and black pepper to taste
¼ teaspoon turmeric
4 bay leaves

Cook lentils in water until tender. Fry onion in margarine and oil until soft and lightly golden. Stir in drained lentils. Mix together ¼ cup milk, 1 beaten egg and bread. Mash with a fork to break up bread. Add remaining ingredients, except bay leaves, and mix well. Add lentil mixture and mix lightly. Turn into a greased Dutch oven (see page 6) and press bay leaves into the top of the dish. Beat remaining 1 cup milk and 2 eggs and pour over. Bake for 1 hour on a grill over medium-hot coals (put coals on the lid of the dish as well).

Vegetarian bobotie with nuts
Serves 6

2 onions, chopped
1 tablespoon margarine
2 cups nuts, very finely chopped (preferably in a blender at home)
1 tablespoon curry powder
1 cup breadcrumbs
2 teaspoons apricot jam
1 teaspoon turmeric
2 tablespoons seedless raisins
1 tablespoon chutney
1 tablespoon vinegar or lemon juice
1 egg, beaten
salt to taste
1 teaspoon yeast extract (Marmite®), dissolved in 1 cup hot water

CUSTARD TOPPING
1 egg
¾ cup milk
salt and pepper to taste
4 bay leaves

Fry onions lightly in margarine. Remove from heat and add remaining ingredients, except hot water and Marmite®. When mixed, gradually stir in the hot water and Marmite®. Place dish in a greased Dutch oven (see page 6).
Prepare the topping by beating the egg, milk and seasonings together. Pour over the nut mixture and insert bay leaves into the bobotie. Cover and place on a grid over medium-hot coals for 1 hour.

Egg curry

Serves 4

1 large onion, chopped
2 tablespoons margarine
1 apple, peeled and diced
¼ cup sultanas
salt to taste
2 tablespoons plain (cake) flour
1 tablespoon curry powder
1 cup milk
½ cup water
2 bananas, quartered
4 hard-boiled eggs, quartered

Fry onion in margarine until golden-brown. Add apple, sultanas and salt. Stir in flour and curry powder. Add milk and water, stirring until sauce thickens. Add bananas and cook gently for 4–5 minutes. Add eggs and serve with rice.

Spiced black-eyed beans

Serves 2–4

1 cup black-eyed beans
4 tablespoons margarine
1 onion, thinly sliced
1 clove garlic, finely chopped
1 tablespoon ground mixed spice
1 tablespoon paprika
½ cup vegetable stock
2 tablespoons tomato purée
2 tablespoons dried parsley

Soak the beans and cook according to the haybox cooking method (see page 7). Heat the margarine in a pan over low heat. Add the onion, garlic, mixed spice and paprika and cook until the onion is soft. Stir in the beans, stock, tomato purée and parsley. Cover and keep on a very low heat for 10 minutes.

Sweetcorn and cheese dish
Serves 4

1 cup creamed sweetcorn
1 cup milk
1 cup breadcrumbs
salt and pepper to taste
1 cup grated Cheddar cheese
½ cup margarine, melted
4 eggs, beaten

Mix all the ingredients together and spoon into a greased, fireproof dish. Cover with lid and bake over low heat (put a few coals on the lid as well), without stirring, for about 40 minutes.

Cheese fondue
Serves 2–4

Buy a packet of pre-packed cheese fondue (available at delicatessens) or prepare your own: grate Gruyère cheese and mix with cornflour (about 2 tablespoons cornflour to 1½ cups cheese). Add a little Kirsch liqueur. Heat slowly until cheese melts. Tear chunks off bread and dip into cheese with a fork. Also delicious with bananas, pineapple and other fresh fruit.

Bread pizza
Serves 4

½ cup cheese spread
pinch of cayenne pepper
4 slices white bread, crusts
   removed
1 x 56 g can anchovies
   (or mussels, asparagus, etc.)
4 tomatoes, sliced
1 teaspoon dried Italian herbs
½ cup grated Cheddar cheese
margarine

Mix cheese spread and cayenne pepper and smear on bread. Arrange anchovies and tomatoes on bread and sprinkle with herbs and Cheddar cheese. Fry the bread in a little margarine until the undersides are toasted and the cheese has melted.

HANDY HINT
To freshen stale bread, sprinkle with water, wrap in foil and place on a grill over medium-hot coals for about 5 minutes, turning frequently.

Burger patties
Makes 8

1 x 120 g packet soya mince,
  curry flavour
1 cup oats
1 teaspoon margarine
4 tablespoons prepared mustard
4 tablespoons chutney

Prepare soya mince according to
the instructions on the packet,
but use only 2 cups of water.
When ready, add oats. Set aside to
allow oats to bind with soya (the
mixture should be quite stiff). As
soon as the mixture is cool enough
to handle, press into patties and
fry in melted margarine until
brown on both sides. Take care not
to break the patties when turning
them. Serve between breadrolls
with mustard or chutney, or on
top of mashed potato.

Mock chicken à la king
Serves 2–4

1 x 37 g packet instant sauce,
  chicken à la king flavour
2 cups milk
1 x 105 g can smoked mussels
  (substitute with mushrooms if
  you don't eat mussels)
1 x 105 g cook-in-the-bag rice,
  chicken almondine flavour

Prepare sauce with the milk,
according to the instructions
on the packet. When ready, add
mussels and stir through. Prepare
rice according to the instructions
on the packet and serve with
the sauce.

Preserves

If you have the time and energy, it will be worth your while to prepare a few preserves at home to be used on safari. Of course glass bottles are always a problem on safari, but if you wrap each one individually, first in a few layers of newspaper (or bubblewrap) and then in a plastic bag, and pack them tightly together in a sturdy trunk, you should not have to worry about the bottles breaking. Remember not to discard the newspaper after you have used a bottle, but wrap it around the empty bottle again and put it back in the trunk so that the other bottles remain tightly packed together.

Spicy onions

2 kg pickling onions
750 g salt
water
5 cups white vinegar
4 teaspoons salt
2 teaspoons ground ginger
1½ teaspoons whole cloves
1½ teaspoons whole allspice
1 cinnamon stick
6 whole peppercorns

Place unpeeled onions and salt in a container. Cover with water and let it stand for 2 days, stirring now and again. Drain and peel onions, taking care to keep the ends intact so the onions don't fall apart. Place onions in a container and cover with boiling water. Leave for 3 minutes, drain and repeat process three times. Spoon onions into warm, sterilized bottles. Put remaining ingredients in a saucepan and simmer for 10 minutes. Cool slightly, strain and pour over onions. Seal bottles and allow to stand for 2–3 weeks before using.

Stewed fruit salad

125 g each dried apricots,
sultanas, dried peaches and
prunes

SAUCE
2 onions, sliced
1 clove garlic, crushed
1 tablespoon oil
2–3 teaspoons curry powder
1 teaspoon turmeric
1½ teaspoons salt
1 teaspoon ground ginger
½ teaspoon grated nutmeg
½ teaspoon ground cloves
1 cinnamon stick
1 whole clove
a piece of lemon rind
1 tablespoon plain (cake) flour
100 ml vinegar
350 ml warm water

Sauté onion and garlic in oil.
Add curry powder and turmeric
and sauté for a further 2 minutes.
Add remaining spices, lemon
rind, flour, vinegar and water
and simmer until sauce thickens.
  Add dried fruit and simmer
until soft. Leave to cool and seal
in sterilized bottles. This salad will
keep for about a year.

Tomato sauce

2 kg ripe tomatoes
2 onions, chopped
2 tablespoons ground allspice
1 teaspoon cayenne pepper
2¼ cups vinegar
1½ cups sugar
4–5 whole cloves
1 teaspoon salt

Dip tomatoes in boiling water,
then peel and chop them into
small pieces. Add remaining
ingredients and cook for 2 hours.
Rub through a sieve or liquidize.
Cook for a further 15 minutes,
then seal in sterilized bottles.

Spicy peaches

2 cups water
1 cup sugar
5 tablespoons vinegar
6 whole cloves
6 allspice corns
2 cinnamon sticks
pinch of salt
small piece of lemon rind
7–9 clingstone peaches

Heat water and sugar until sugar dissolves. Add remaining ingredients, except peaches, and boil for 1 minute. Add peaches and simmer for 20 minutes, or until peaches are soft. Remove lemon rind. Leave to cool, spoon into sterilized bottles and seal. Use within six months.

> **VARIATION**
> Other fruit such as bananas, peaches and prunes can also be preserved in this way.

Curried beans

2 kg fresh green beans
1 kg onions, finely chopped
3 cups vinegar
1½ cups sugar
2 tablespoons curry powder
3 tablespoons cornflour

Top-and-tail beans and cut them smaller if preferred. Cook the beans in a little salted water, drain, then add onions, 2 cups vinegar and all the sugar and bring to the boil. Mix the curry powder and cornflour with 1 cup vinegar and add to the beans. Stir until the cornflour is cooked. While still hot, pour into sterilized jars and seal.

Curried fish

3 kg fish (kingklip, red roman,
  geelbek or kabeljou)
milk and plain (cake) flour to
  coat fish
oil

SAUCE
6 onions, sliced
2 tablespoons oil
2 tablespoons curry powder
1 teaspoon turmeric
2 whole cloves
¼ teaspoon grated nutmeg
2 teaspoons cornflour
1 teaspoon brown sugar
6 bay leaves
1 fresh chilli, crushed
salt to taste
6 peppercorns
2 cups vinegar

Cut fish into portions, dip in
milk, then in flour and fry in
hot oil. Drain on paper towel.
Pack fish into sterilized bottles.
   To prepare the sauce, sauté
onions in oil until soft. Add
curry powder, turmeric, cloves and
nutmeg and sauté for 3 minutes.
Add remaining ingredients and
simmer for 20 minutes. Pour hot
sauce over fish and allow to cool.
Seal and leave for at least 2 days
before eating.

Peach chutney

1.5 kg peaches, finely chopped
750 g onions, finely chopped
3 cups brown vinegar
1 cup sugar
1 cup apricot jam
salt to taste
1 tablespoon curry powder
1 tablespoon turmeric
1 tablespoon ground allspice
1 teaspoon ground cloves
1 tablespoon ground coriander
2 fresh chillies, chopped

Mix all the ingredients together
and simmer for 2 hours. Pour into
sterilized bottles and seal.

Pasta

Mediterranean macaroni
Serves 6

2 cups macaroni
1 onion, chopped
1 tablespoon margarine
2 cups cooked and diced
  chicken
1 cup canned peas
1 x 410 g can mushroom soup
½ cup milk
1 cup chopped salami
½ cup black olives
1 teaspoon salt
1 cup grated Cheddar cheese

Cook macaroni in salted
water until soft. Sauté onion
in margarine, then mix with
remaining ingredients, except
the cheese. Spoon into a greased,
fireproof dish and top with cheese.
Place over medium-hot coals for
about 30 minutes.

Macaroni al tonno
Serves 4

2 cups macaroni
3 tablespoons oil
1 onion, chopped
1 green pepper, seeded and
  chopped
1 cup tomato juice
1 tablespoon lemon juice
black pepper to taste
1 x 210 g can tuna, drained
  and flaked
6 anchovies, mashed
1 tablespoon capers (optional)
6–8 black olives, stoned

Cook macaroni in salted water
until soft. Heat oil in a pan and
fry onion and green pepper until
soft. Add tomato juice, lemon
juice and seasoning, and bring to
the boil. Simmer for 10 minutes.
Add tuna, anchovies, capers and
olives and heat through. Spoon
over macaroni.

Macaroni and cheese
Serves 4

2 cups macaroni
1 tablespoon margarine
1 cup white sauce (see page 93)
½ cup canned peas
3 rashers bacon, cut into small
  pieces and fried until crisp
1 tomato, sliced
1 cup grated Cheddar cheese

Cook macaroni in salted water until soft. Drain and mix with margarine. Add white sauce, peas and bacon and mix well. Put in a greased Dutch oven (see page 6) and arrange tomato slices on top. Sprinkle with cheese. Cover with lid and bake over low-heat coals until cheese has melted.

Lasagne
Serves 4–6

1 tablespoon oil
500 g beef mince
1 x 68 g packet minestrone
  soup
1 x 410 g can tomato and
  onion mix
¼ cup water
lasagne sheets, or other noodles
¼ cup margarine
½ cup plain (cake) flour
4 cups milk
1 teaspoon salt
pinch of pepper
1 cup grated Cheddar cheese

Heat oil and brown mince. Add soup powder, tomato and onion mix and water. Cook for 5 minutes. Cook noodles in salted water until soft. Melt margarine and add flour, stirring constantly to prevent lumps. Gradually stir in milk and simmer for 3 minutes, stirring constantly. Add seasoning.

Arrange half the lasagne in a greased Dutch oven (see page 6). Spoon half the mince over and cover with half the sauce. Repeat layers. Top with cheese. Cover and place on a grid over low heat for about 45 minutes (remember to put coals on the lid as well).

Pasta with beans and onion relish
Serves 6

3 cups penne pasta
3 cups green beans

ONION RELISH
2 tablespoons oil
1 onion, sliced
⅓ cup white vinegar
⅓ cup dry red wine
⅓ cup brown sugar

Add pasta to a large pan of boiling, salted water. Boil, uncovered, until soft. Drain. Slice beans to resemble shape of penne pasta, then boil in salted water until just tender. Drain and mix lightly with pasta.

To prepare the relish, heat oil in a pan and fry onion until light brown. Add remaining ingredients and simmer uncovered for 10 minutes. Spoon over the pasta and beans.

Pasta with mushrooms and tuna
Serves 4

2 cups pasta
1 clove garlic, crushed
1 teaspoon oil
1 tablespoon margarine
2 tomatoes, chopped
1 cup chopped mushrooms
1 x 210 g can tuna, drained
   and flaked
pinch of cayenne pepper
1–2 anchovies (optional)

Cook pasta according to the instructions on the packet, drain and keep warm. Sauté garlic in oil and margarine. Add tomatoes and simmer for 10 minutes. Add mushrooms, tuna and cayenne pepper and simmer for a further 10 minutes. Mix sauce with pasta and garnish with anchovies.

Pasta with green pepper
Serves 6

1 x 250 g packet macaroni
2 green peppers, seeded and
  sliced
1 clove garlic, crushed
2 tablespoons olive oil
1 x 410 g can whole tomatoes,
  chopped
½ teaspoon salt
¼ teaspoon black pepper
½ cup grated Parmesan cheese

Cook pasta according to the
instructions on the packet, drain
and keep warm. Fry green pepper
and garlic in olive oil. Remove
from oil. Add tomatoes to oil and
simmer for 10 minutes. Season
and mix with green pepper and
garlic. Stir into pasta and sprinkle
with cheese.

Spaghetti with mussels
Serves 4

1 x 500 g packet spaghetti
3 tablespoons oil
1 clove garlic, crushed
1 x 410 g can mussels on
  the half shell, drained
  (reserve liquid)
pinch of black pepper
1 tablespoon dry white wine

Cook spaghetti according to the
instructions on the packet, drain
and keep warm. Heat olive oil,
garlic and reserved liquid from the
mussels and simmer very gently
for about 5 minutes. Add pepper,
white wine and mussels and
simmer for a further 10 minutes.
Mix with spaghetti and serve.

Bread, Scones, Vetkoek and Batters

Irish potato bread
Serves 4

150 g (about 2) medium
  potatoes
1 tablespoon margarine
1 teaspoon salt
plain (cake) flour

Wash potatoes and cook in skins
until soft. Drain and leave to cool.
Peel and mash with margarine,
salt and enough flour to make a
pliable dough. Knead on a board
sprinkled with flour. Roll out until
12 mm thick. Cut into wedges and
bake on a greased, hot grid over
hot coals or in a greased, heavy-
based saucepan until brown on
both sides.

Health bread
Makes 2 loaves

2 heaped teaspoons bicarbonate
  of soda
6 tablespoons honey
3 x 500 ml tubs natural yoghurt
6 cups nutty-wheat flour
4 cups bread flour
1½ cups bran
salt to taste

Mix bicarbonate of soda and
honey with yoghurt. Add to the
dry ingredients and mix well. The
dough must not be too stiff. Bake
for 1½ hours, or until ready, in a
greased Dutch oven (see page 6).

Chapatis
Makes 6

2 cups nutty-wheat flour
1 teaspoon salt
¼–½ cup water
oil for frying
margarine or butter

Blend the flour and salt with just enough water to form a stiff dough. Knead the dough until smooth and elastic. Place in a mixing bowl and cover with a damp towel. Allow to rest for 2–3 hours.

Knead the dough once more and divide into 6 equal pieces, each about the size of an egg. Shape each piece into a flat, round patty and roll out thinly until about 150 mm in diameter.

Heat the oil in a heavy-based frying pan and fry each chapati until brown spots appear on the side being fried. Flip and repeat. Remove from heat and spread margarine on one side. Wrap the chapatis in a clean tea towel to keep them soft and warm. Spread lightly with margarine or butter and serve.

Indian coconut bread
Makes 6 cakes

½ cup desiccated coconut
½ teaspoon salt
½ cup plain (cake) flour
pinch of cayenne pepper
½ teaspoon castor sugar
2½ tablespoons water
½ cup oil for frying
margarine or butter

Place dry ingredients in a bowl. Mix in the water and blend to form a fairly stiff dough. Divide the dough into 6 equal portions and shape each into a flat patty about 75 mm in diameter. Heat the oil and fry the coconut cakes carefully until golden-brown on both sides. Drain on absorbent paper towel. Spread lightly with margarine or butter and serve.

Easy onion bread
Makes 1 loaf

1 x 58 g packet onion soup
water
1 x 175 ml tub natural yoghurt
1 x 500 g packet self-raising
   flour

Mix onion soup with a little water
to form a smooth paste. Add
yoghurt and self-raising flour. Put
dough in a small, greased Dutch
oven (see page 6) and bake for
30–45 minutes.

Beefy potbread
Makes 1 loaf

1 x 500 g packet self-raising
   flour
1 x 68 g packet oxtail soup
pinch of cayenne pepper
½ cup grated Cheddar cheese
2 cups buttermilk

Mix all the ingredients together
to form a dough and place in a
greased Dutch oven (see page 6).
Bake for about 1 hour, or until
bread is ready.

Fried potbread
Serves 4

2 cups plain (cake) flour
1 tablespoon baking powder
½ teaspoon salt
1 cup water (more may be
   needed)
2 tablespoons oil

Mix the flour, baking powder
and salt and add water gradually
to form a smooth dough. Form
the dough into round balls and
flatten them with your palms. Fry
in heated oil for about 10 minutes
per side, or until golden-brown.

Sweetcorn bread
Makes 1 loaf

1 x 410 g can creamed
   sweetcorn
salt and pepper to taste
2 tablespoons margarine,
   melted
4 eggs, beaten
½ x 500 g packet self-raising
   flour

Mix sweetcorn, seasoning and
margarine with the eggs. Stir in
the flour and mix until smooth.
Put into a small, greased Dutch
oven (see page 6) and bake over
hot coals for 1 hour.

Potbread 1
Makes 1 loaf

1 x 500 g packet self-raising
  flour
1 teaspoon salt
1 tablespoon ground ginger
½ cup margarine
1 x 397 g can condensed milk
¼ cup milk
2 tablespoons granulated yeast
a little tepid water
1 tablespoon sugar

Mix self-raising flour, salt and
ginger with margarine. Add
condensed milk and milk. Mix
yeast with water and sugar. Leave
to stand for a few minutes, then
add to flour. Mix until smooth. Put
dough in a small, greased Dutch
oven (see page 6). Put in a warm
place and allow dough to rise.
Cover and place pot on coals (put
a few coals on the lid as well). Bake
until bread sounds hollow when
tapped (about 30–45 minutes,
depending on the heat of the coals).

Potbread 2
Makes 1 large or 2 small loaves

6 cups plain (cake) flour
1 tablespoon salt
2 teaspoons castor sugar
1 x 10 g packet instant yeast
7 tablespoons margarine
1 cup lukewarm milk
¾ cup lukewarm water

Combine flour, salt, sugar and
yeast in a bowl. Melt margarine
in milk and add, with water, to
dry ingredients. Mix thoroughly
and knead until dough is elastic
and no longer sticks to your hand.
Place in a greased Dutch oven (see
page 6). Leave dough to rise in a
warm place until it has doubled in
size. Cover and place pot on a grid
over moderate coals (put a few
coals on the lid as well). Bake for
about 1 hour, or until bread
sounds hollow when tapped.

Ashcakes 1

Serves 4–6

1 x 500 g packet self-raising
  flour
½ teaspoon salt
¼ cup margarine
½ cup buttermilk

Mix flour and salt, then rub in
margarine with fingers. Add
buttermilk and mix to form a
pliant dough. Form dough into
balls and press flat with your
palms. Put each cake onto a piece
of foil. Close foil securely, but
leave space for the air to expand.
Place on low coals and turn from
time to time. Bake for about
15 minutes, or until ashcakes
are done.

> **HANDY HINT**
> To toast bread, simply arrange slices
> of bread on a grill over very hot
> coals. Be careful not to burn the
> bread – turn slices with a long fork
> or metal tongs when light brown
> on one side.

Ashcakes 2

Makes 1 cake

1 cup self-raising flour
1 teaspoon baking powder
1 teaspoon salt
¼–½ cup water
1 tablespoon margarine or oil

Mix flour, baking powder and salt.
Heat water and margarine (or oil)
and mix with flour mixture to
form a soft, pliable dough. Form
into a round ball and flatten with
your palms. Put dough directly on
top of low coals and bake for
about 30 minutes. Shake well to
get rid of the ash before eating.

Beer bread

Makes 1 loaf

1 x 500 g packet self-raising
  flour
1 teaspoon salt
¼ cup oil
1 x 340 ml can beer

Mix flour and salt together. Add
oil and beer and mix well. Knead
until smooth and put dough into
a small, greased Dutch oven (see
page 6). Bake over hot coals for
about 1 hour.

Spicy bread

Cut bread into slices, smear with crushed garlic, margarine and salt, or a mixture of grated cheese and Marmite®. Wrap bread in foil and place on a grill over hot coals until margarine or cheese has melted.

Rusk bread
Makes 1 loaf

2½ tablespoons granulated
  yeast
½ cup lukewarm water
1 x 397 g can condensed milk
1 x 500 g packet self-raising
  flour
1 teaspoon salt
¼ cup margarine, melted

Mix yeast with water and condensed milk and leave to stand for a few minutes. Mix with flour and salt and knead until smooth. Leave to stand for about 10 minutes to rise. Break off small pieces of the dough and shape into rusks. Smear each piece with margarine and pack, standing, next to each other in a greased Dutch oven (see page 6). Bake over hot coals for 1 hour.

Quick bread mix
Makes 3 loaves

1.5 kg white bread flour
4 teaspoons salt
1½ teaspoons bicarbonate
  of soda
4 teaspoons baking powder
1 tablespoon cream of tartar
1¼ cups coffee creamer
500 g (1 brick) margarine

Mix the dry ingredients together in a large mixing bowl. Cut in the margarine with a knife, then rub it in to form a crumbly mixture. Place in a large, airtight container and store in a cool, dry place for up to three days. When you are ready to bake the bread, simply add enough water to achieve the correct consistency, place the dough in a greased Dutch oven (see page 6) and bake for about 1 hour. The mix is also suitable for stick bread (see page 114).

Frypan corn bread
Serves 2

1 cup mealie meal
1 cup plain (cake) flour
2 tablespoons sugar
1 teaspoon salt
2 teaspoons baking powder
2 eggs, beaten
4 tablespoons margarine,
  melted
1 cup milk

Combine the dry ingredients.
Blend the eggs, margarine and
milk. Quickly mix everything
together and pour the batter into
a warm, well-greased frying pan.
Cover and place immediately
over low heat to bake for about
45 minutes.

Fried oatmeal bread
Serves 4–6

1½ cups plain (cake) flour
2 teaspoons baking powder
¼ teaspoon salt
½ cup margarine
8 tablespoons oats
2 teaspoons sugar
1 cup milk (or a little less)
oil for frying

Mix the flour with the baking
powder and salt and rub in the
margarine. Stir in the oats and
sugar. Make a well in the centre
and add enough milk to make
a soft dough. Break off pieces
of dough, roll between your
palms (flour them first) and
flatten to form cakes. Fry in an
oiled frying pan until golden-
brown on both sides.

Stick bread
Makes 4–6

2 cups quick bread mix
  (see page 113)
¼ cup water
margarine

Mix the bread mix to a soft
dough with the water. Mould
small quantities of dough into
spirals around skewers or clean
sticks (not dry ones or they will
catch fire – also make sure the
sticks are not from poisonous
trees). Make sure the dough covers
the end of the stick so it won't slip
off. Bake on a grid over low coals
for 15–20 minutes, turning often.
Slip the bread off the stick and
serve with margarine in the hollow.

Griddle cakes
Makes 10

1 x 500 g packet self-raising
   flour
1 teaspoon salt
1 egg
¼ cup oil
milk
water

Mix the flour and salt together.
Break the egg into a cup and
add oil. Fill the cup with an
equal mixture of milk and water.
Whisk the mixture thoroughly
and mix it with the flour and salt.
Form balls and press between your
palms to flatten slightly. Heat a
griddle and bake over moderate
coals for 15 minutes, turning once.

Knapsack cookies
Makes 15

2 cups oats
pinch each of salt and
   bicarbonate of soda
1 tablespoon margarine, melted
warm water
margarine

Mix oats, salt and bicarbonate
of soda with melted margarine
and enough warm water to bind
the mixture. Knead into a round
shape and press to 10 mm thick
on a flat surface sprinkled with
oats. Cut into squares and bake
on a grid over hot coals until the
sides begin to brown. Turn over
to brown the other side as well.
Spread with margarine.

Vetkoek
Makes 10–15

1 cup plain (cake) flour
1 teaspoon baking powder
½ teaspoon salt
1 egg, beaten
½ cup water
oil for frying

Mix the dry ingredients together.
Mix the egg and water and add
to the flour. Mix together to form
a soft dough. Place tablespoon
measures in hot oil and fry,
turning once, until golden-brown
on both sides.

Green mealie bread

5–6 green mealie cobs
2 eggs, beaten
½ teaspoon salt
2 tablespoons sugar
2 teaspoons baking powder

Cut the kernels from the cobs
and place in a basin, together with
the eggs. Add the salt, sugar and
baking powder and mix well. If the
mixture seems too stiff, add some
water to form a soft dough. Place
the mixture in a small, greased
bowl or tin that is opened at
one end. Cover with a piece of
greaseproof paper and stand the
bowl or tin in a pot with enough
water to come halfway up the
bowl. Cover the pot and allow the
water to simmer for 2 hours. If
you have used a tin, cut open the
other end and push out the bread.

Crumpets
Makes 30

2 cups plain (cake) flour
2 tablespoons baking powder
2 teaspoons salt
2 tablespoons sugar
1 egg
2 cups milk
2 tablespoons oil
margarine

Mix flour, baking powder and
salt together and add sugar. Beat
egg, milk and oil together, pour
into flour mixture and mix well
to form a thin, smooth batter.
Fry tablespoon measures of the
batter in a little margarine until
golden-brown on both sides.

Batter for fritters

1 cup plain (cake) flour
pinch of salt
½ cup milk
2 eggs, separated

Mix flour and salt, and add milk
and egg yolks, stirring well to
make a smooth batter. Fold in
stiffly-beaten egg whites. Add thick
slices of fruit, Wiener sausages or a
filling of your choice and fry each
slice separately in hot oil until
golden-brown.

Pancake batter
Makes 12

4 eggs
a little less than ½ cup water
½ cup oil
½ teaspoon salt
1 cup milk
1¾ cups self-raising flour
oil for frying

Whisk eggs and water together.
Add oil, salt and milk and, lastly,
the flour. Beat slowly until mixture
is smooth. Fry pancakes in oil.

Scones
Makes 10

2 cups whole-wheat flour
3 teaspoons baking powder
pinch of salt
3 tablespoons margarine
1 egg, beaten
1 tablespoon honey
  (or golden syrup)
milk

Mix together dry ingredients, then
rub in the margarine. Add egg,
honey and enough milk to make a
fairly soft dough. Press out lightly
and cut into rounds with a glass or
cup. Place in a greased Dutch oven
(see page 6) over moderate coals
(put a few coals on the lid as well)
for about 15 minutes, or until
scones are baked.

Cheese scones
Makes 10

½ cup finely chopped onions
2 tablespoons margarine
¼ cup plain (cake) flour
½ teaspoon salt
1 teaspoon baking powder
6 eggs
2 cups grated Cheddar cheese
oil for frying

Fry onion in margarine. Mix
flour, salt and baking powder
together. Beat eggs well and add
cheese, dry ingredients and onion.
Mix lightly and fry tablespoon
measures in hot oil until brown
on both sides.

Desserts

Pineapple pan pudding
Serves 4

½ cup margarine
4 tablespoons brown sugar
4 rings canned pineapple
¼ cup white sugar
2 eggs, beaten
8 tablespoons self-raising flour
pinch of salt
cream

In a frying pan, mix together 4 tablespoons margarine with the brown sugar. Melt, but do not allow the mixture to boil. Lay the pineapple rings in the pan. Cream the rest of the margarine with the white sugar until creamy and smooth. Stir in the eggs, then the flour and salt. Spread mixture over the pineapple rings, cover the pan tightly and cook over very low heat for 30 minutes. Turn onto a plate so that the pineapple is on top, and serve with cream.

Ginger delight
Serves 6–8

2 x 200 g packets ginger biscuits
¼ cup custard powder
2 cups water
1 cup golden syrup
½ teaspoon ground ginger
1 tablespoon margarine

Break biscuits into small pieces and place in a greased container. Dissolve custard powder in a little water. Add rest of water to custard powder and cook for 4 minutes over moderate heat. Add syrup, ginger and margarine and mix well. Pour over biscuits and leave to cool completely. Serve in container or turn out onto a plate.

Peach marshmallows
Serves 4

1 x 410 g can peach slices, drained
1 cup marshmallows, cut into small pieces

Turn peaches into a heatproof serving dish and sprinkle marshmallows over the top. Warm a metal sheet over the fire and carefully place it over the dish (make sure there is no ash or dirt on the sheet) until the marshmallows are grilled and melted.

Chocolate apple pudding
Serves 4

1 x 425 g jar apple purée
½ cup cream, whipped
plain chocolate, grated

Spoon the apple purée into a serving dish and cover with whipped cream. Sprinkle chocolate over the top.

Jam ping-pongs
Serves 4

2 cups self-raising flour
8 tablespoons margarine
pinch of salt
water
raspberry jam (or any other flavour)
whipped cream or custard

Mix the flour, margarine and salt together in a bowl and add enough water to make a rather stiff dough. Roll between floured palms to form balls the size of a ping-pong ball. Make an indentation in the centre of each one and insert some jam, sealing it over afterwards. Cook in boiling water for about 15 minutes and serve with whipped cream or custard.

Traditional malva pudding
Serves 10

1 cup sugar
2 eggs
3 tablespoons apricot jam
2 cups plain (cake) flour
2 teaspoons baking powder
pinch of salt
2 teaspoons bicarbonate of soda
2 cups milk

SYRUP
½ cup margarine
2 cups sugar
1 cup boiling water
2 teaspoons vanilla essence
   or brandy
2 cups milk
pinch of salt

Beat the sugar and eggs together
until creamy. Add jam, flour,
baking powder and salt. Mix
bicarbonate of soda with milk
and add to the pudding mixture.
Spoon the mixture into a greased
Dutch oven (see page 6) and bake
for 1 hour over moderate coals
(remember to put coals on the
lid as well).
   To make the syrup, melt the
margarine, then stir in the
remaining ingredients. Heat,
but do not boil.
   When the pudding is baked,
slowly pour over the syrup,
allowing it to soak into the
pudding before serving.

Lemon foam pudding
Serves 4

3 oranges
juice and grated rind of
   1 lemon
3 eggs, separated
4 teaspoons sugar
2 teaspoons cornflour

Squeeze enough juice from the
fruit to make 1 cup, adding water
if necessary. Put egg yolks, sugar,
cornflour and fruit juice in a
saucepan. Add the lemon rind.
Cook over low heat, stirring.
Increase heat and bring to the boil
just long enough to let it thicken.
Beat the egg whites until stiff, and
fold into the sauce. Can be served
warm or cold.

Bread pudding 1
Serves 4

2 cups white breadcrumbs
(stale bread works best)
3 cups warm milk
2 eggs
½ cup sugar
¼ cup margarine, melted
½ teaspoon salt
1 teaspoon vanilla essence
apricot jam

Soak breadcrumbs in the milk
and leave to cool. In a separate
bowl, whisk the eggs and sugar
together, then add the remaining
ingredients. Add to the bread and
milk and pour the mixture into a
greased Dutch oven (see page 6).
Cover and place on a grid over low
heat (put a few coals on the lid
as well). Bake for approximately
1 hour, or until the pudding has
set. Serve with apricot jam.

Bread pudding 2
Serves 4–6

2 cups milk
¼ cup margarine
¼ cup white sugar
1 cinnamon stick
pinch of salt
2 eggs, lightly beaten
½ cup seedless raisins
2 tablespoons apricot jam,
heated slightly
3 cups brown or white
breadcrumbs

Heat, but do not boil the milk,
margarine, sugar, cinnamon
and salt. Remove from heat and
gradually add the mixture to the
eggs. Mix well and add raisins,
jam and breadcrumbs. Pour into
a greased Dutch oven (see page 6)
and bake for about 1 hour.

Apple fritters

Serves 4

4 large apples, peeled, cored
   and cut into 5 mm thick rings
½ cup sugar
icing sugar

BATTER
1½ cups plain (cake) flour
¼ teaspoon salt
1 tablespoon oil
1 egg, separated
¾ cup milk
oil for deep-frying

Dip apple rings in sugar and leave
to dry slightly on paper towel.

Prepare the fritter batter by
mixing flour and salt together in
a bowl. Make a well in the centre
and add the oil and egg yolk.
Gradually draw the flour into the
egg, adding the milk a little at a
time, beating to produce a smooth
batter. Whisk the egg white until it
stands in firm peaks and fold into
the batter mixture.

Heat the oil and coat apple rings
in batter. Fry for about 4 minutes
or until golden and cooked
through. Drain on paper towel and
sprinkle with icing sugar.

Fruit fritters

1 cup plain (cake) flour
¼ teaspoon salt
1 egg
⅘ cup milk
1½ teaspoons baking powder
fruit such as bananas, peaches,
   pineapple, pears, apples
   (fresh or canned)
oil for frying
cinnamon sugar

Mix the flour and salt together.
Whip the egg and milk together
and add it gradually to flour. Stir
in baking powder and mix well.
Cut fruit into bite-size pieces
and stir it into the batter. Fry
tablespoon measures in hot oil,
turning frequently to ensure
that the fritters are cooked on
all sides. Drain on absorbent
paper towel before serving with
cinnamon sugar.

Souskluitjies
Serves 4

1 cup plain (cake) flour
1 teaspoon baking powder
¾ teaspoon salt
4 tablespoons margarine
2 eggs
1 tablespoon sugar
water
¼ teaspoon ground cinnamon
cinnamon sugar
another 4 tablespoons
   margarine, melted

Mix flour, baking powder and
¼ teaspoon salt together. Rub
in 4 tablespoons margarine. Whisk
eggs and sugar until creamy. Add
to flour mixture and mix lightly.
Pour water into a small saucepan
until it is about 5 cm deep and
add cinnamon and remaining salt.
Bring water to the boil and add
teaspoon measures of the batter
(not more than 4 or 5 dumplings
at a time). Simmer gently for
about 10 minutes. Lift dumplings
out of water with a slotted spoon,
put in a bowl and keep warm over
a pot of boiling water. Sprinkle
with cinnamon sugar and melted
margarine. Repeat process until
batter is finished.

Rice dumplings
Serves 6

1 cup rice, uncooked
4 tablespoons plain (cake) flour
1 teaspoon baking powder
½ cup seedless raisins, chopped
pinch of salt
2 eggs
water
cinnamon sugar
2 tablespoons margarine,
   melted

Boil rice in lightly salted water
until soft. Drain and leave to cool.
Mix flour, baking powder, raisins
and salt and add to rice. Whisk
eggs and add to rice. Form mixture
into small balls and roll each ball
in flour. Fill a saucepan halfway
with water and bring to the
boil. Add dumplings and cover
saucepan. Boil for approximately
15 minutes. As soon as dumplings
float, they are ready. Remove and
sprinkle with cinnamon sugar and
melted margarine.

Pudding-in-the-pot 1
Serves 6–8

SYRUP
4 cups water
1 cup sugar
¼ cup golden syrup
2½ tablespoons margarine
1 teaspoon vanilla essence

BATTER
¼ cup golden syrup
2½ tablespoons margarine
½ cup milk
¼ cup brandy
1 teaspoon bicarbonate of soda
1 cup plain (cake) flour
2½ tablespoons cocoa powder
pinch each of ground ginger,
    grated nutmeg and salt

To prepare the syrup, place all ingredients in a large saucepan, cover and bring to the boil.

To make the batter, melt syrup and margarine in a separate saucepan, then remove from heat. Mix the milk, brandy and bicarbonate of soda, then add the remaining ingredients. Add the mixture to the melted syrup and margarine.

Place spoonfuls of the batter in the boiling syrup, cover and boil slowly for about 30 minutes, or until cooked. Do not lift the lid during cooking. Serve hot with custard.

Pudding-in-the-pot 2
Serves 6–8

5 cups water
2 cups sugar
2 cups plain (cake) flour
2 teaspoons ground cinnamon
1 teaspoon ground ginger
½ teaspoon salt
2 tablespoons apricot jam
2 tablespoons margarine
¾ cup milk
2 teaspoons bicarbonate of soda

Bring water and sugar to the boil in a large, covered saucepan. Mix flour, cinnamon, ginger and salt together. Rub jam and margarine into flour mixture. Mix milk and bicarbonate of soda and add to other ingredients. Pour batter into boiling syrup and cook on high heat, covered, for 5 minutes. Move saucepan to low heat and cook slowly for another 25 minutes, without lifting the lid.

Lemon crunch
Serves 4

4 tablespoons castor sugar
2 tablespoons cornflour
1 x 410 g can evaporated milk
½ cup boiling water
2 eggs, separated
grated rind and juice of
  1 lemon
ginger biscuits, crushed
pieces of chocolate flake

Mix sugar with cornflour and
blend with evaporated milk.
Gradually stir in water. Pour into
saucepan and bring to the boil,
stirring. Simmer 5 minutes, then
remove from heat. Beat egg yolks,
add and return saucepan to heat.
Cook for 2–3 minutes, stirring,
but do not boil. Add lemon juice
and rind and remove from heat
to cool. Beat egg whites to soft
peaks and fold into the mixture,
blending well. Spoon into
individual dessert bowls with
alternate layers of biscuit crumbs.
Top with chocolate flake.

Grilled bananas

For each serving, use 1 firm,
unpeeled banana. Place bananas
on a grill over medium-hot coals
and leave for about 8–10 minutes,
turning frequently. Serve hot with
honey or cinnamon sugar.

Trifle
Serves 6–8

1 Swiss roll or sponge cake
  (a packet of Boudoir® biscuits
  may also be used)
1 cup custard, warmed
1 cup fruit juice
1 cup chopped fruit
  (fresh or canned)
1 cup cream
2 tablespoons sugar
½ teaspoon vanilla essence

Cut cake into slices and pack into
a dish. Spoon over half the custard,
then half the fruit juice and fruit.
Repeat layers. Beat the cream,
sugar and essence together and
spoon on top of the trifle.

Mango trifle
Serves 8

2 packets Boudoir® biscuits
1 x 410 g can mangoes, drained
  (reserve syrup)
¼ cup custard powder
2¼ cups milk
3 tablespoons sugar
½ cup cream, whipped
chocolate, flaked or grated

Line a flat-bottomed dish with
a layer of biscuits. Pour mango
syrup over. Mix custard powder
with a little milk until smooth.
Bring remaining milk to the boil
and add custard. Add sugar and
simmer for 1 minute over low
heat. Pour half the custard over
the biscuits while still hot. Chop
mangoes into small pieces and
arrange on top of custard. Place
another layer of biscuits in the
dish and pour over remainder
of hot custard. Leave to cool
completely and decorate with
cream and chocolate.

Pear condé
Serves 4

1 x 410 g can pear halves, sliced
3 teaspoons cornflour
1 x 425 g can cooked rice
  pudding

Measure ½ cup juice from the
pears. Mix with cornflour and
bring to the boil. Simmer gently
for 4 minutes. Turn the rice
pudding into a serving dish,
arrange the pears on top and
glaze with the sauce.

Banana flambé
Serves 4

½ cup margarine
¾ cup sugar
2 teaspoons lemon juice
¼ cup brandy
6 bananas
cream

Melt margarine in a large pan
and add sugar, lemon juice and
half the brandy. Cut bananas
in half lengthways and arrange
in a pan. Simmer until sauce
turns brown and bananas are
slightly cooked. (Be careful not
to overcook bananas.) Heat
remaining brandy, ignite it and
pour over bananas while still
flaming. Serve with cream.
(Bananas can be replaced by
other fresh or canned fruit.)

Cool pear dessert
Serves 8–10

1 x 825 g can pear halves,
  drained (reserve syrup)
1 x 80 g packet lemon jelly
½ cup boiling water
1 x 410 g can evaporated milk
custard (optional)

Mash pears very finely with a
fork. Dissolve jelly in boiling water
and leave to cool. Add 1½ cups
pear syrup to jelly (make up with
water if syrup is not enough). Pour
jelly and evaporated milk into a
mixing bowl, together with the
mashed pears, then whisk for a
few minutes. Pour mixture into
a mould that has been rinsed
with cold water and place in a
refrigerator or cooler box until
set. Turn out onto a plate and
serve on its own or with custard.

HANDY HINT
Clean out plastic 1-litre milk (or
fruit juice) bottles, fill them with
water and freeze. Useful to keep in
the cooler box as they stay cold much
longer than commercial freezer
blocks, and you have ice cold water
with your sundowners when you get
to camp and the water has defrosted.

Easy dessert
Serves 6

1 x 1-litre container instant
  custard
apricot jam or caramel
  condensed milk
1 packet Marie® biscuits

Heat custard until very hot.
Sandwich jam or condensed milk
between biscuits and arrange in
a flat dish. Pour hot custard
over biscuits and allow to cool.
Crumble a few biscuits over the
top for decoration.

Filled peaches
Serves 4–6

1 x 410 g can peach halves,
  drained (reserve syrup)
1 cup minced mixed fruit
  mixture
¼ cup brandy
cream

Fill peach hollows with fruit
mixture and pack into a heavy,
flat-bottomed saucepan. Pour
peach syrup over peaches and
place saucepan over medium
heat for about 15 minutes. Heat
brandy, ignite and pour over
peaches. Serve with cream.

Rice pudding 1
Serves 4

¼ cup rice, uncooked
pinch of grated nutmeg
1 piece of lemon rind
2 teaspoons lemon juice
1 packet instant caramel
    pudding
2 cups water
2 tablespoons sugar
¾ cup evaporated milk
½ teaspoon vanilla essence
2 teaspoons margarine
1 tablespoon seedless raisins
1 tablespoon sultanas
3 tablespoons dried apricots,
    chopped
½ cup cream, whipped
custard

Cook rice, nutmeg, lemon rind,
lemon juice and caramel pudding
powder in water until rice is soft.
Add sugar, evaporated milk and
vanilla essence and cook for a few
more minutes. Add margarine,
raisins, sultanas and apricots and
cook for another 3 minutes. Leave
to cool slightly and stir in cream.
Remove lemon rind and serve
warm with custard.

Rice pudding 2
Serves 6

2 cups cooked rice, cooled
2 cups thick cream
½ cup seedless raisins
jam (any flavour)

Mix rice and cream with the
raisins and a serve cold with a
dollop of jam on top.

Apple crisp
Serves 4–6

1 x 785 g can apples, drained
    (reserve syrup)
2 tablespoons margarine
2 tablespoons golden syrup
2 cups Rice Crispies®
1 cup cream, lightly whipped

Mash apples very finely with a
fork. Melt margarine and apple
syrup and add apples, syrup and
Rice Crispies®. Mix well and
spoon into a dish, alternating
layers of apples and cream. Chill
well before serving.

Vanilla delight
Serves 6

1 packet Tennis® biscuits
½ cup sweet wine
1 x 90 g packet instant vanilla
  pudding
1 cup cold milk
1 cup cream, whipped
¼ teaspoon vanilla essence

Arrange biscuits in a flat-bottomed serving dish and sprinkle with wine. Whisk instant pudding in cold milk (add another ½ cup if mixture seems too thick) and, as soon as it starts to thicken, add the cream and vanilla essence. Spoon onto biscuits and decorate with biscuit crumbs. If possible, serve chilled.

Apples in foil

1 apple per person, washed
  and cored
soft brown sugar
margarine

Make a cut in the skin all the way round the apples with the point of a knife. Fill cavities with sugar and place a small piece of margarine on each apple. Fold securely in foil and place in embers for 30–45 minutes.

Strawberry milk jelly
Serves 4

1 x 80 g packet strawberry jelly
1 x 410 g can evaporated milk
bananas to decorate

Dissolve jelly in enough boiling water to cover, and stir until jelly is dissolved. Make up to 1¼ cups with cold water. When jelly is on the point of setting, whisk in enough evaporated milk to make up to 2½ cups, or slightly less in hot weather. Whisk well and turn into a serving dish to set. Decorate with sliced bananas.

Caramel bake

Serves 6

1 teaspoon bicarbonate of soda
½ cup milk
2 cups apricot jam
½ cup margarine
1 cup plain (cake) flour
pinch of salt
2 eggs

SAUCE
2 cups milk
1 x 397 g can caramel
  condensed milk
¼ cup brandy

Dissolve bicarbonate of soda in milk and add apricot jam. Rub margarine into flour and salt with fingers. Add bicarbonate of soda mixture to flour. Beat eggs and add to mixture. Place in a Dutch oven (see page 6).

To prepare the sauce, heat milk and condensed milk and add brandy. Pour over batter. Cover and bake pudding for about 30–45 minutes over medium heat (put a few coals on the lid as well).

Syrup dumplings

Serves 6

3 cups self-raising flour
½ teaspoon salt
2 teaspoons margarine
milk

SYRUP
3 cups boiling water
1 cup sugar
2 tablespoons golden syrup
juice and grated rind of
  1 lemon

Sift flour and salt and rub in margarine. Mix in enough milk to make a stiff batter.

To make the syrup, boil all the ingredients in a large saucepan.

Put tablespoon measures of the batter into the boiling syrup, put the lid on and cook gently for 20 minutes without lifting the lid.

Chocolate mousse
Serves 6

1 x 125 g packet marshmallows
1 x 200 g slab plain chocolate
1 x 410 g can evaporated milk, chilled

Melt marshmallows and chocolate in a container over a pot of boiling water, stirring from time to time. Whisk the evaporated milk until thick (add a dash of lemon juice to speed up the process). Remove marshmallows and chocolate from heat as soon as they are melted and add the evaporated milk. Mix thoroughly and leave in a cool place to set.

Apricot yoghurt
Serves 4–6

1 x 80 g packet apricot jelly (substitute with peach if apricot is unavailable)
1 cup boiling water
2 cups apricot or peach yoghurt
custard

Dissolve jelly in boiling water and allow to cool completely. Stir in yoghurt and place in the refrigerator or cooler box to set. Serve with custard.

Banana and guava dessert
Serves 6–8

1 packet Marie® biscuits
1 x 397 g can caramel condensed milk
2 x 410 g cans guava halves, drained (reserve syrup)
6 bananas, sliced and sprinkled with lemon juice
2 cups thick custard
1 cup cream, whipped
nuts, chopped

Arrange a layer of biscuits in a flat-bottomed dish. Beat the condensed milk until smooth and spoon over the biscuits. Top with another layer of biscuits. Pour the guava syrup over the biscuits. Chop the guavas and spoon over the biscuits. Arrange the bananas on top and cover with custard. Decorate with cream and nuts.

Cottage cheese pudding
Serves 6–8

1 Swiss roll or sponge cake
  (buy ready-prepared, or
  substitute with a packet
  of Boudoir® biscuits)
1 x 250 g tub smooth
  cottage cheese
1 x 397 g can condensed milk
¼ cup lemon juice
1 x 410 g can youngberries,
  strawberries or guavas
1 tablespoon custard powder

Cut cake into slices and arrange
in flat-bottomed dish. Beat
together the cottage cheese,
condensed milk and lemon juice
and leave for a while to thicken.
Spoon over cake slices. Simmer
fruit (if guavas are used, chop
them finely), including the syrup,
with the custard powder until
sauce thickens. Allow to cool
and then spoon over cottage
cheese mixture.

Chocolate pudding
Serves 6

¼ cup margarine
1 cup sugar
1 teaspoon vanilla essence
1 egg, beaten
1 cup self-raising flour
2½ tablespoons cocoa powder
¼ cup milk
1½ cups boiling water

Mix margarine, ½ cup sugar
and vanilla essence together until
creamy. Stir in egg. Stir in flour,
1½ tablespoons cocoa powder
and the milk. Pour mixture into
a greased Dutch oven (see page 6).
Mix remaining sugar and cocoa
and sprinkle over the batter. Pour
over boiling water. Put lid on
saucepan, cover with foil and bake
in the ground for about 1 hour.

Guavas with chocolate biscuits
Serves 6

1 x 820 g can guava halves,
  drained (reserve syrup)
1 packet Chockits® biscuits
custard

Remove pips from guavas with a teaspoon, and add pips to syrup (whisk with a fork to mix syrup and pips). Press a chocolate biscuit into the guava hollows and arrange in a flat-bottomed, heatproof dish. Pour the guava syrup over the biscuits. Cover dish with a lid or foil and place on a grid over low heat for about 10 minutes until lukewarm. Serve with custard.

Apples with cornflakes
Serves 4–6

2 tablespoons margarine
1 tablespoon brown sugar
1 tablespoon golden syrup
pinch of ground cinnamon
2 cups cornflakes
1 x 765 g can apples

Melt margarine, sugar and syrup together and add cinnamon and cornflakes to mixture. Heat apples in their own liquid, then drain most of the liquid and arrange apples in a serving bowl. Spoon the cornflake mixture over the apples and serve hot.

Easy Rice Crispies® dessert
Serves 4

1 x 397 g can caramel
  condensed milk
1 tablespoon lemon juice
3 cups Rice Crispies®

Beat condensed milk and lemon juice together until smooth. Add Rice Crispies® and mix well.

VARIATIONS
Replace the Rice Crispies® with cornflakes, or replace the caramel condensed milk with either plain condensed milk or instant custard.

Ginger apples
Serves 6

¼ cup golden syrup
½ cup ginger biscuits, crumbled
½ cup seedless raisins
2 tablespoons brandy
   (preferably ginger brandy)
6 apples, cored
margarine

Mix syrup, biscuits, raisins and brandy. Fill apples with mixture. Put a small knob of margarine on top of each apple, wrap in foil and bake in the embers for 20 minutes, or until apples are soft.

Honeyed pears
Serves 4

1¼ cups water
¼ cup brown sugar
grated rind and juice of
   1 lemon
3 tablespoons honey
4 pears, peeled

Boil water, sugar, lemon juice and rind and honey together. Add pears and simmer slowly until soft, basting pears all the time. As soon as pears are soft, remove them and boil sauce until it becomes syrupy. Spoon syrup over pears, then serve.

Pears in red wine
Serves 8

8 firm pears
juice of 1 lemon
1 bottle red wine
1 cinnamon stick
4 whole cloves
¼ cup sugar
grated rind of 1 orange
cream

Peel the pears and brush with lemon juice. Pour the wine into a saucepan and add the remaining ingredients, except the cream, together with the pears. Gradually heat the wine and simmer gently until the pears are soft (be careful of overcooking). It is important to constantly pour wine over the pears and to turn them over a few times to make sure they cook evenly. When the pears are soft, remove them and boil the wine until it reduces to a syrupy glaze. Spoon the syrup over the pears and serve with cream.

VARIATION
Instead of wine, use cider or apple juice and add a berry jam to make the juice syrupy.

Cakes and Sweet Nibbles

Toffee crispies

¼ cup margarine
¾ cup sugar
1 x 397 g can condensed milk
1 tablespoon golden syrup
1 teaspoon vanilla essence
2 cups Rice Crispies®

Melt margarine and sugar together.
Add condensed milk and syrup
and slowly bring to the boil.
Simmer for 20 minutes, stirring
continuously. When mixture
reaches soft-ball stage (measured
by dropping a teaspoonful of the
mixture in a cup of cold water – if
it forms a soft ball, it is ready), add
essence and Rice Crispies®. Pour
mixture into a greased container
and cut into squares when cold.

Date crisps

1½ cups dates, pitted and
   chopped
2 tablespoons margarine
1 cup sugar
1 egg, beaten
3 cups Rice Crispies®
½ cup desiccated coconut

Boil all the ingredients together
for 5 minutes, except the Rice
Crispies® and coconut. Remove
from heat, add Rice Crispies®
and press into a greased container.
Sprinkle with coconut and cut into
squares when cold.

Dried fruit bars

1 cup oats
1 cup Rice Crispies®
1 cup All Bran Flakes®
1 cup desiccated coconut
1 cup dried prunes, chopped
½ cup dried apricots, chopped
½ cup margarine
¾ cup soft brown sugar
1 x 397 g can condensed milk

Mix oats, Rice Crispies®, All Bran Flakes®, coconut, prunes and apricots in a bowl. In a saucepan, mix margarine, sugar and condensed milk and stir over low heat until the sugar is completely dissolved. Add condensed milk mixture to dry mixture, mix thoroughly and press into a greased container. Refrigerate for a few hours before cutting into bars.

Fudge

3 cups sugar
¼ teaspoon salt
1 cup thin cream
1 cup desiccated coconut
1 teaspoon vanilla essence

Mix sugar, salt and cream together and heat slowly until sugar has dissolved completely. Add coconut and simmer slowly for 10 minutes, stirring from time to time. Remove from heat and add vanilla essence. Pour into a greased container and cut into squares when cold.

Breadnuts

6 slices stale bread
1 plateful sugar water
1–2 eggs
1 tablespoon sugar
1½ teaspoons plain (cake) flour
2 tablespoons chopped nuts
oil for frying

Dip the bread quickly in the sugar water. Mix remaining ingredients, except oil, and smear it on bread. Heat oil and fry each slice for 2 minutes on each side, or until golden-brown. Cut bread into quarters and leave to cool before serving.

Standard pie crust

1 packet Marie® or Tennis®
  biscuits
4 tablespoons margarine,
  melted
3 tablespoons sugar

Put biscuits in a large, strong
plastic bag and close bag securely,
making sure all the air is squeezed
out. Roll biscuits with a rolling
pin or any round container
(a bottle works well) until finely
crumbled. Pour crumbs into a
bowl and add margarine and sugar.
Mix very well. Press mixture into
the bottom and against the sides
of a flat-bottomed container and
fill with desired filling.

Caramel filling

1 x 90 g packet instant
  caramel pudding
1–1½ cups cold milk
6 dates, chopped
8 glace cherries, chopped
¼ cup walnuts, chopped
¼ cup watermelon jam
½ cup cream, stiffly whipped

Mix the caramel pudding with
the milk and beat until thick.
Mix in all the other ingredients,
except the cream. Spoon into pie
crust (see pie crust recipe, this
page) and decorate with cream.
Refrigerate and serve.

Almond tart filling

1 cup margarine
¾ cup sugar
1 cup oats
pinch of salt
1 egg, beaten
1 teaspoon almond essence
apricot jam

Melt margarine and sugar together.
Add oats, salt and egg and stir for
5 minutes over low heat. Add
almond essence. Smear apricot
jam over the bottom of pie crust
(see pie crust recipe, this page)
and pour mixture on top. Leave
to cool before serving.

Pineapple tart filling

1 small pineapple, grated
½ cup water
1 cup sugar
2 teaspoons margarine
1 egg, separated
¼ teaspoon salt
1½ tablespoons cornflour

Mix pineapple with water, sugar, margarine and beaten egg yolk and cook for 10 minutes over very low heat. Add salt. Stir cornflour, which has been blended with a little cold water, into the pineapple mixture. Simmer until mixture is thick and cooked, stirring continuously. Remove from heat. Fold in stiffly beaten egg white and pour mixture into a pie crust (see page 137). Allow to cool before serving.

Pineapple milk tart

1 small pineapple, grated
2 cups water
1 x 80 g packet pineapple jelly
1 x 397 g can condensed milk

Boil pineapple in 1 cup of water for 10 minutes. Dissolve jelly in 1 cup of boiling water and add to the pineapple. Mix well and leave to cool. Add condensed milk and mix well. As soon as mixture starts to thicken, pour into a pie crust (see page 137) and leave in a refrigerator or cooler box to set.

Custard tart

⅔ cup lemon juice
1 x 397 g can condensed milk
2 tablespoons custard powder
2 cups milk
⅔ cup sugar
2 teaspoons margarine
1¼ packets Tennis® biscuits

Beat the lemon juice and condensed milk together. Mix custard powder with milk and sugar and simmer for 7 minutes over low heat until custard is cooked. Add margarine and allow to cool. Pack a layer of biscuits in a flat-bottomed dish and pour condensed milk and lemon juice over the top. Arrange another layer of biscuits on top and pour custard over. Decorate with banana or peach slices or crumbled biscuits. Leave to cool before serving.

Marshmallow tart

1 x 250 g packet marshmallows
1 x 250 g chocolate slab
  with nuts
½ cup milk
1 cup cream, stiffly whipped

Melt marshmallows and chocolate
in a bowl of milk placed over
boiling water, stirring frequently.
Leave to cool slightly and add
cream. Spoon into a pie crust
(see page 137) and leave in a
cool place until set.

VARIATIONS
1. Replace cream with a can of
   evaporated milk.
2. Serve without a pie crust as
   chocolate mousse or in pear
   halves for dessert.

Peanut squares

20 cream crackers
1 x 397 g can caramel
  condensed milk
1 x 250 g packet salted peanuts

Crush biscuits finely and mix with
the other ingredients. Press into a
greased container and place in a
refrigerator or cooler box to set.
Cut into squares.

Fruit and nut bars

¼ cup margarine
1 x 250 g packet soft
  marshmallows
¾ cup Rice Crispies®
½ cup dried apricots, finely
  chopped
¼ cup unsalted peanuts

Melt margarine in a pan, add
marshmallows and stir until
melted. Add Rice Crispies®,
apricots and peanuts and mix well.
Transfer mixture into a shallow,
square dish and press down gently
with a hot metal spoon. Cut into
squares when cool.

Savoury Nibbles

Biltong squares
Makes 18 small squares

½ cup smooth cottage cheese
1½ tablespoons mayonnaise
pinch each of salt and pepper
4 slices bread, crusts removed
2 cream crackers (or more if
   the bread slices are large)
biltong, finely grated

Mix cottage cheese, mayonnaise
and seasoning, and smear it on
both sides of the bread slices.
Sandwich the cream crackers
between the slices of bread. Cut
into squares and roll in biltong.

Nibbler's treat
Makes 7 cups

5 tablespoons margarine
5 tablespoons oil
2 chicken stock cubes
2 teaspoons curry powder
½ teaspoon ground ginger
½ teaspoon peri-peri
3 cups Rice Crispies®
2 cups cornflakes
2 cups puffed wheat

Melt margarine in oil. Add stock
cubes and stir until dissolved. Add
curry powder, ginger and peri-peri.
Mix in cereals and stir well. Leave
to cool before serving.

Porridge snacks

Prepare porridge according to the recipe on page 18.

Form porridge into balls and roll first in beaten egg and then in breadcrumbs mixed with either dried herbs or Parmesan cheese. Fry porridge balls in hot oil until golden-brown.

VARIATION

Press porridge around a cube of cheese and wrap a piece of bacon around it. Secure with a toothpick and grill over hot coals until bacon is crisp.

Cheese balls
Makes 15

3 egg whites
2 cups grated Cheddar cheese
pinch of cayenne pepper
½ cup chopped ham (or salami,
  beef, prawns, mushrooms)
oil for deep-frying

Beat egg whites until very stiff. Fold in cheese, cayenne pepper and ham. Using two spoons, place small quantities of the mixture in hot oil and deep-fry until golden-brown. Drain on absorbent paper towel and serve hot or cold.

HANDY HINT

To keep food warm, place the covered saucepan on the ground close to the fire, and turn it around now and again. Be careful not to kick dirt into the pan. Alternatively, put a saucepan with boiling water on the fire and place the food in another dish that fits snugly over the saucepan. Cover food with a lid or foil. This is an ideal way to keep food such as toast and fritters warm.

Index

Index